The Lost Art of House Cleaning

A Clean House is a Happy Home

Enjoy the Clean
Jan / Head rag
Dragger

D1457842

Jan M. Dougherty
the "Head Rag Dragger"

Outskirts Press, Inc.
Denver, Colorado

Author's Note:
No suggestions, methods or materials mentioned in this book is warranted or guaranteed. All products, methods and suggestions are the based on the author's own personal experience. As with any new suggestions it is judicious to perform a spot test on any material or finish. As I tell my employees, 'when in doubt, proceed with caution or do nothing'.
JMD, HRD

Outskirts Press, Inc.
http://www.outskirtspress.com

ISBN: 978-1-4327-6712-9

Outskirts Press and the "OP" logo are trademarks belonging to Outskirts Press, Inc.

PRINTED IN THE UNITED STATES OF AMERICA

Table of Contents

Nitty Gritty Index

Index of Photos

Preface

I've owned a residential cleaning company for six years and I've come to the conclusion that the art of housecleaning has all but been lost. I believe I may be the only survivor who knows how to clean and therefore I have a duty and responsibility to pass on my wisdom (and share the pain) before it's too late.

I was taught to clean while quite young from my mother who was born in Italy; that alone should tell you a whole lot. I was the only girl out of four children so you know I got the graduate level, intensive version of how to clean. Don't get me wrong, my brothers were also taught to clean and we were all expected to take care of our room or else; but as my mother explained to me, the only girl, "you're going to get married and have a family, if you don't know how to take care of a house properly, you're going to be living in a pig sty and I won't visit you". Hmmmmm!

When I tell people I love to clean they think I wasn't even lucky enough to get rocks for brains, but I love my house when it's clean and shiny and smells clean. When my home is clean I feel good. I believe a clean house makes for a happy home and a happy homeowner. I also enjoy a good challenge – when I'm done cleaning its Jan – 1, Dirt – 0!

I have a collection of books with hundreds of helpful hints on how to clean this or that. Some are just wonderful, well written and very informative, how to clean vomit, blood, strained peas, what have you. They give recipes for cleaning mixtures, but some of the components I still haven't found. Their lists are alphabetical, or by material type, or by type of stain, say puke; dog puke, cat puke, baby puke, praying to the porcelain God puke or just plain old puke puke. These books are good, but they still don't tell you how to actually clean *the whole house* from start to finish.

In these last six years I've cleaned more houses that looked clean on the surface, but were actually dirty once we got down to the nitty-gritty. I've also cleaned lots of houses that were just plain dirty. This, by the way, isn't a criticism, for my business and the 12 women that work for me this is job security.

While doing my estimate I'd point out to the customer what we would clean and how we would do it and I was always surprised by the customers' reactions. They didn't know the stove could be pulled out or that the knobs came off the stove or that the microwave could be dismantled. They hadn't known to clean the vent on the bottom of the refrigerator or vacuum the coils behind the vent. Or that silk plants and trees can be washed. Too many of my customers were stunned by the scope of the job I was proposing and skeptical I could deliver what I was promising. But this is how I've been cleaning my whole life.

My next clue that everyone doesn't clean like I do was when I started hiring employees. My first two employees had been cleaning house for other people for years and were quite confident that they could do what I wanted until I started the training!

I showed them that with only three products and a small assortment of tools they could clean the world and everything in it and then I showed them The PATH! "Who taught you to clean this way?" "Wow, you should write a book about this". "I can't wait to get home and do this to my own house"; which, by the way, they all did soon after learning The PATH.

So I've written this book and here it is. At first glance it may look intimidating, but if you kick back, put your feet up and maybe pour yourself a nice glass of iced tea or wine and read it the first time for entertainment. You might just want to read it a second time for inspiration and then it could be You -1; Dirt – 0!

Introduction

I've come to the conclusion that most people who claim to hate house cleaning hate it simply because they don't know how. They think about cleaning their house or even a room but are overwhelmed with where to begin, how to clean some of the stuff they have; or how to get from here to there and *be done* with the job.

Chances are good they were never formally *taught* just what to do or how to do it. I was, trust me, and I was grounded until I got it right. Also, as teenagers most of you were probably too busy being just that, a teenager (snot-nosed, know it all) and that included not paying attention when your mother had tried to teach you how to clean your room or you simply refused to learn and your rooms looked like the pig sties that my mother warned me about. Of course, you figured you'd marry someone with enough money so you wouldn't have to clean, but that didn't happen, so now you're going to have to do it yourself.

Another reason you may not have learned to clean was your mother was made to clean by *her mother* when she was a teenager and so she swore she wouldn't do *that to any of her kids!* Hence, here you are an adult; mother, father, homeowner and you are totally unprepared to keep a house (clean). You haven't the foggiest idea how to do what you know needs to be done.

I'd be willing to bet that, for a good number of you reading this book, when your mom comes to visit she spends most of the time cleaning, straightening and rearranging your house. She may have something to say about this and doesn't hesitate to point out to you what your shortcomings are; or she may say nothing and suffers in silence wondering where she went wrong.

Let's look at it this way; no one is at fault that you don't know how to clean your house because until now; this book didn't exist! And, trust me, for all the how-to books out there I still haven't found one that describes the *actual* process of cleaning the *whole house.*

Fear not, faint soul, there is light at the end of the tunnel and it is not the light of an oncoming train. There is system, a methodology to cleaning. There is a way; you start here, you end there. I call it The PATH. Follow me my child and I will show you The PATH.

The objective of this book is to give you a list of products and tools, what to use on what, when to use it and describe The PATH, which is step-by-step, room-by-room directions to get "it" done and done right. The Nitty Gritty at the end of the book will be quite extensive because it will give detailed instructions on cleaning specific items or pieces of furniture so as to not muddy the momentum of The PATH.

I will attempt to get you as excited about cleaning your house as I am. It's not the cleaning that's exciting it is the satisfaction for having done the job, sometimes a hard job, well. When you master the basics you'll be able to whip through the house in no time (but first turn the TV off) and finish with the satisfaction that *you did what had to be done and you won!* You – 1; Dirt – 0!!

So ladies and gentlemen, boy and girls, you are about to embark on a journey, a journey to the heights and depths of your house, a journey that may change your life! But then again it may not!

All together now, "Let's do Dirt"!

Love,
Jan
the "Head Rag Dragger"

CHAPTER 1

Cleaning Products And Tools

This chapter lists everything you will ever need to do any cleaning job for the rest of your life. I have added a second copy of this list in the back of the book so you can tear it out and take it with you when you go shopping. The pages right after this list is an explanation of each item, pictures where necessary, where to get them, how much you'll need and how to use them. There are a few additional things that I have not included here but they are dictated by circumstances *and are not critical* to getting the job done, I will explain them when the occasion arrives or in The Nitty Gritty.

CLEANING PRODUCTS

- **Krud Kutter** – 1 Gallon
- **White Vinegar** - 1 Gallon
- **Soft Scrub with Bleach** – one

TOOLS

- **Spray bottles** (9) - I buy the cheapies ($.98)
- **White terry cloth rags** (5 doz.) - Sam's Club in packages of 60
- **Microfiber rags** (4 doz.) - Sam's in packages of 24
- **Small detail brush** – Paint dept. hardware store

- ➢ **Medium detail brush** – You can find these anywhere
- ➢ **Scotch Brite Scouring Pads** (NO sponge) – Sam's
- ➢ **Pumice Stone** – Get the one *without* handle
- ➢ **Grit cloth** – Looks like window screen, but is not
- ➢ **Vacuum** – I use both a canister and upright
- ➢ **Webster** – Extendable pole with round brush
- ➢ **Swiffer Sweeper (X Large)** - Buy online or in store
- ➢ **Swiffer Dusters** (w/extension handle) - any store
- ➢ **Divided caddy** – this is simply for convenience
- ➢ **Plastic pitcher** – any size over 1.5 quarts
- ➢ **Ladder/step stool** – how tall you are and what you have in your house will determine the sizes you'll need
- ➢ **Tool kit** – You need a few screwdrivers and needle nose pliers. I also use dental tools to get into some tight places, but these are optional
- ➢ **Shower Curtain** – New and plastic
- ➢ **BUCKET** – *FORBIDDEN!*

KRUD KUTTER ($13-16/gal) (Photo 1.1)

No, this is not a joke. This stuff is really called Krud Kutter. And, it Kuts the Krud! It is a biodegradable, nontoxic degreaser that does not eat my hands like a lot of other degreasers that I've used. I clean bare-handed; I don't use gloves, because I need to be able to feel the dirt since I can't always see it. For the rest of this document when I'm referring to Krud Kutter it will be KK for full strength and KK5/1 for the dilution.

Photo 1.1
Krud Kutter

You'll find KK at Home Depot, Lowes and Wal-Mart; but you will find it in the Paint Department, not where you would look for cleaning stuff. In Ace, it's in the cleaning aisle. If you don't find it at a store near you go online to: www.krudkutter.com.

When I moved from Georgia to Arizona I couldn't find it in any store so I called the company and they directed me to a local Ace Hardware. Buy it by the gallon; don't bother with the smaller bottle. Before I started using it in my business and just cleaned my house a gallon lasted about 1 year. So, over the long haul it's a pretty good deal.

The KK is used both full strength and diluted 5 parts water; 1 part KK. **When you make the dilution put the water in the spray bottle first then the KK. Otherwise, you make bubbles and won't be able to get the water in.**

WHITE VINEGAR ($2 gal)

Use the vinegar to clean everything you didn't clean with the KK and also to 'finish' after you have used the KK on cabinets, floors and kitchen/bath appliances. Use it on metal, ceramic, baskets (yes, baskets), fabrics (yes fabrics too), wood, silk plants (OMG! definitely on silk plants), knick knacks and do-dads. We're talking 100% white vinegar and **do not** dilute it.

SOFT SCRUB with BLEACH (Hereafter: SS/B)

You'll find it in the cleanser section of (insert your store's name) duh! This is used primarily on porcelain fixtures; tubs, toilets, showers, and sinks both kitchen and bathroom. If you don't like the smell of bleach on your hands I'd suggest using gloves with this stuff. Also make sure you're wearing a light colored shirt or an old rag that you don't care about because it will take the color out of whatever it touches. NEVER, NEVER use a Microfiber rag when using SS/B!

SPRAY BOTTLES

Get the cheapest bottles wherever you can. Why 9 of them you ask? Because you'll need 9! I'll explain why in more detail when we get to do the actual job and how 9 spray bottles fit in the maintenance program. You're going to have to mark them so you know which is which; KK, KK5/1 and vinegar. We have ours color coded. Each bottle has colored duct tape around the neck of the bottle and on the sprayer. Keep it simple and be consistent.

WHITE TERRY CLOTH RAGS (Hereafter referred to as WTR)

I get mine at Sam's; they are in the Auto Department (don't ask why, I don't know). Buy yourself 5 dozen. They come in packages of 60 rags for $18.00, so there's your 5 dozen. Wash and dry them before you use them the first time because they have sizing in them and won't work right out of the bag. Use your rags with abandon. As soon as your rag gets "wet" or dirty throw it down and get a clean one.

For those of you who are into 'living green' these rags will last years and can be used in place of paper towels. Wash them, bleach them and use them until they fall apart.

MICROFIBER RAGS (Hereafter referred to as **MFR**)

I also get these at Sam's; they are in the Auto Department too! Your guess is a good as mine why, but it doesn't matter. They come in packages of 24 for just under $10.00. (That's about $.42/rag – Cheap!!) Stay away from the fluorescent yellow ones; they just **look dirty** even after you wash them. You may think they are expensive, but over time when you see how they clean you won't whine about what you paid for them. They're just magic when it comes to cleaning. Again, you have to wash and dry these before you use them for the first time. No cheating either – wash them. Do not use these on anything that is greasy or absolutely filthy or with bleach. Use the WTR to clean something and 'finish' with the MFR (more about 'finish' in The Nitty Gritty). These are what you'll use in the maintenance plan too.

NOTE: Do not, I repeat DO NOT wash the WTR with the MFR. Trust me, been there, done that. The WTR lint gets on the MFR and it's a nightmare to get off; especially when the MFR are new.

SMALL DETAIL BRUSH (Photo 1.2)

I find these in the paint department of hardware stores. Typically, they are black, look like toothbrushes and have 3 different types of bristles; two are metal of some kind and one is not – get the one that is *not* metal; get several they're small and relatively cheap. Now guess what you do with a detail brush? You do detail! You'll use these all over the house in just about every room.

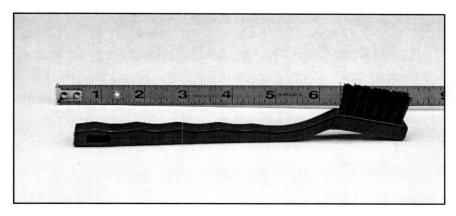

Photo 1.2
Small Detail Brush

MEDIUM DETAIL BRUSH (Photo 1.3)

These are in just about every store. It is not a scrub brush. It should have a handle long enough for you to get a good grip on it and give you some leverage.

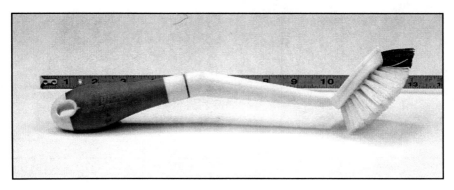

Photo 1.3
Large Detail Brush

7

SCOTCH BRITE SCOURING PADS (Photo 1.4)

We call these things "green scrubbies". They are green and we use them to scrub, hence our name for them. If you happen to find the large sheets about (6x9) cut them into 4 pieces (at Sam's again). They are easier to work with when smaller and when it no longer does the job for you; toss it.

These are expensive (my opinion) if you buy the package of 3 that you find in most stores. I buy mine at Sam's and I can get 20 (6x9) sheets for $6.34. After I cut each sheet in 4, I end up with 80 pads. They now cost $.08 (yes, that's 8 cents) per pad – *big* price difference.

Photo 1.4
Scotch Brite Pads: Large 6x9 sheet cut in 4 pieces

Photo 1.5
Pumice Stone

PUMICE STONE (Photo 1.5)

I prefer to buy the stones ***without*** the handle. The one we use is slightly longer than a stick of butter and not much bigger around. The material seems to be softer and you can break it in half so it's easier to maneuver in the toilet. This is how you get the mineral/water ring out of the toilet. Cleanser ain't gonna do it!

GRIT CLOTH (Photo 1.6)

It is just what the name implies. You can find these in with the sandpaper section in hardware stores where it's called Drywall screen. They are about 4 x 11, 2 sheets in a package. Cut these into 4-5 pieces. I also use grill/griddle screens which I buy at an industrial/commercial cleaning supply store. I cut these in half. Cut whatever you get into a manageable size and throw it out when it gets limp and doesn't seem to be doing the job.

DANGER! DANGER! WILL ROBINSON! The grit cloth can be dangerous if not used with great delicacy. You can rub right through the porcelain finish of a fixture with these and then you have to either replace it or live with it. These are used on mineral deposits in and around bathroom and kitchen fixtures. Before you use one of these make sure you understand that you have a weapon in your hands and if you don't feel comfortable don't do it. I will not replace your sink or tub if you destroy it using one of these things.

Photo 1.6
Grit Cloth

VACUUM(S) (Photo 1.7)

Yes, the (s) implies plural. I have 7 Oreck upright and canister units that I use in my business. For the work we're doing, the Oreck makes the grade because it is so light and I like the replaceable filters. I use a canister with all the attachments; hose, 2 poles (or wands), crevice tool, round brush (I prefer the horsehair brush, it does not mash down like the synthetic bristle brush), upholstery tool and 2 floor tools. One floor tool comes with the unit, the black one in the photo is optional, but I recommend it if you have both hard floors and carpets/rugs in your house. I also use the upright vacuum.

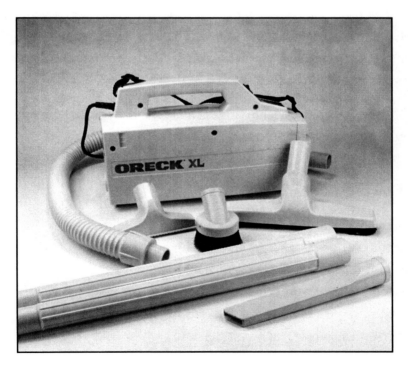

Photo 1.7 A
Canister Vacuum with standard attachments

Photo 1.7B
The black floor piece is will clean both carpeting and hard floors.
Purchased separately

If you only have an upright I hope you have the attachments listed above. If you do not, you will be in a world of hurt trying to get to the cooties. But you'll see what I mean as you read the chapters where I describe the cleaning in detail.

If you have an upright with the attachments you can get by but I might suggest you purchase a "Webster".

WEBSTER (Photo 1.8)

The Webster is a full round brush on a pole that extends. We use this to get into the high places that we can't reach with the canister with both poles and crevice tool even on a ladder. When you use your Webster, if you are feeling left out of the experience you can make vacuuming sounds while dusting. I have found these in the mop/broom section of stores. This can be purchased on line at www. acehardwareoutlet.com.

Photo 1.8
Webster

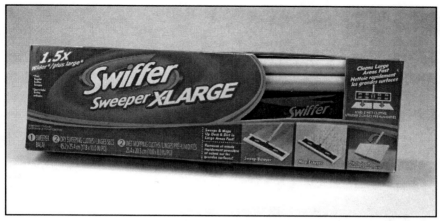

Photo 1.9
Swiffer X-Large Mop

SWIFFER SWEEPER MAX/SWIFFER SWEEPER X-LARGE
(Photo 1.9)

We use the Swiffer Sweeper Max/Swiffer Sweeper X-Large because the head is so much bigger than that little teal colored swiffer most people have and it is the perfect size for the WTR we use with them.

The Swiffer Max and Swiffer X-Large are identical except for the packaging. I've been purchasing the Max at <u>acehardwareoutlet. com</u> on line because they disappeared from the stores. However, I just found them at <u>swiffer.com</u> under the label Swiffer X-Large. At this site they give you a list of stores that are *supposed* to be carrying them or where you can buy them online. It appears to me that they took the Swiffer Max and repackaged it as the Swiffer X-Large, because they *are* identical, I've purchased both. The costs differ slightly between vendors so you make the call.

Photo 1.10
Swiffer Duster

SWIFFER DUSTERS (Photo 1.10)

If you don't already have a swiffer you should buy a starter kit. I prefer the wand that extends and bends. This is necessary for maintenance.

DIVIDED CADDY (Photo 1.11)

This is purely for convenience. The one shown in photo is stocked as if I am about to clean. It's handy for dragging around your tools; spray bottles, brushes, grit cloth, scrubbie, etc. You don't *need* one – but I can't imagine doing the job without it. It's also good for all those little things you find while you're down on your knees. Hey, you can only fit so much of that trash in your pockets.

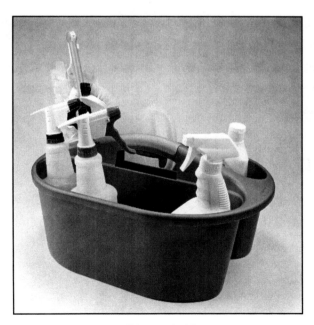

Photo 1.11
Divided Caddy loaded, ready to go to work.

PLASTIC PITCHER

We use the pitcher to rinse shower/tub walls so the size isn't that important. Ours are about 1.5quart size. You can also use it to mix a batch of Margaritas in it when you're finished.

LADDER/STEP STOOL

When doing the big job you need to be able to get to the top of all your furniture; china cabinets, bookcases, top of kitchen cabinets and pot shelves around rooms, also for taking down all that stuff high on your walls. Ideally, when on the ladder or step stool the top of the piece you are cleaning should be *at or below your armpits*. The tops of these places need to be *cleaned* so you need to be able to see what you're doing as well as reach them. You also need to reach any ceiling fans you have. We're not cleaning just the blades but the fan motor too (That big round thing above the blades). That's probably dirtier than the blades, since I'm sure, you have not cleaned that when you've dusted the fan blades (You *have* dusted the fan blades, haven't you?)

TOOL KIT

We have small tool kits with several different screwdriver tips that we use when we take the kitchen apart. They do not have to be of any high quality, just functional.

SHOWER CURTAIN

Buy the cheapest shower curtain you can find, it must be plastic. You will use this to cover the floor or furniture below any high things you are cleaning. Also, for those who do not have any space outside your house to put things to dry, you can use this space.

BUCKET

Remember the bucket. ***There will be no buckets.*** Raise your right hand, put your left hand over your heart and repeat 10 times: *I will never use a bucket cleaning house again.* All jobs both the big job and maintenance will be spray and wipe. If you do have a bucket put the book down now and go throw it out. There are several reasons for the NO BUCKET RULE. First; the first time you rinse your rag or mop in the bucket you now have a bucket of dirty water. How do you clean with dirty water? I personally haven't figured that one out. Second, with the amount of space you'll be covering, especially for the big job, by the time you finish one room you will have a full blown case of tendonitis in your wrists from wringing out the rags. (Stop reading and imagine wringing out a rag, now imagine doing this a couple hundred times. Now imagine yourself paralyzed for the next week or two until the inflammation goes down.) Therefore - no rag wringing. (Say that fast 10 times).

That's pretty much it. The few other things I use are more for special circumstances and I will explain them as they happen or in The Nitty Gritty.

CHAPTER 2

Stuff You Need To Know Before You Begin!

THERE ARE ONLY 2 TYPES OF CLEANING

When you "clean" your house each week or month or whenever you get around to it, for the most part, you are doing *maintenance cleaning.* You straighten the place up (I hope) then you dust, vacuum or mop. You do this week after week, month after month and maybe even year after year. Well, what I want to know is when do you do the other half of the job, the *BIG JOB?* (Also, referred to as the BJ)

THE *BIG JOB*

"What, pray tell, is the *BIG JOB"* you ask? It's what you haven't been doing but which desperately needs to be done. Maintenance cleaning is only one-half the job; the other half is the *"BIG JOB"*.

Depending on what part of the country you come from, you would call it the Spring Clean, a deep clean, or a whole house clean. Where I came from we called it the Spring Clean even when we did it in November. Everything in the house gets cleaned. When possible every piece of furniture is moved and cleaned behind, under and all around. Every knick-knack is washed, blinds taken down, mattresses turned, get my drift? The whole enchilada is cleaned.

The beauty of the "*BIG JOB*" was that after it was done, then the maintenance was a skate. You can only pick up, straighten and "dust" for just so long, then it's gotta be *cleaned*.

The air we breathe has oil, or grease, in it, especially in the kitchen and the rooms nearest the kitchen. This air and what's in it (greasy dirt) lands on everything; it does not discriminate, it lands on ceramics, fabric, wood, painted wood, silk flowers, straw flowers, and pictures. Did you know the back side of pictures hanging on your walls is just as dirty as the front? Take one down and check it. Everything gets dirty and the dirt builds up. With time you notice that after you've dusted something it still 'looks' dull. It just doesn't shine anymore, for that matter it hasn't shined for quite a while. If you dusted it and it didn't look clean and shiny, then –Taa Daa! It's still dirty!

Look around your house. Do you have any silk plants? Are the green parts still green all the way down to the base of the stem? Or do they have this gray cast to them in general, and are white the closer to the base you get. Spit on your finger and rub the leaf, especially near the base of the leaf. Did any dirt come off? If you now have a clean spot on the leaf the plant needs to be cleaned. Does the glass in your pictures hanging around your house shine? Is the glass silky to the touch? Run your hand over the glass; is it slick? No, then it needs to be cleaned and the back is just as dirty. Trust me.

So, the *BIG JOB*, usually done at least once a year, depends on your particular circumstances; like how many kids or animals do you have and your personal threshold for dirt. Other considerations are: Do you live in the country or city? Is your maintenance schedule weekly, less than once a month, or hit and miss? Hey, it's your dirt, your house, you make the call. Of course, you could be looking around your house right now and thinking "this place isn't too bad". Hey, all I can say is, thanks for at least buying my book.

THERE ARE ONLY THREE TYPES OF ROOMS

Really! There is the kitchen; this is easily recognized because it usually has a sink, stove, refrigerator and maybe a dishwasher and is used primarily to prepare food.

Then there is the bathroom; this has at least one sink, toilet and tub or shower. Some bathrooms may have more than one of any of these things but that's your problem.

Then there is the "Other"; which is any room that *is not* a kitchen or bathroom. And here you thought you had more rooms than that.

The PATH to clean these three types of rooms is essentially the same; with slight variations due to what is built in and the kinds of dirt you'll find in them.

WHAT YOU ARE *NOT* GOING TO DO

Remember whenever you're doing the *BIG JOB* you **DO NOT** go into any drawer, closet, cabinet or door. Please read that sentence several more times. Closets, cabinets, drawers are a whole other bag of snakes to save for another day. We are cleaning the house; not cleaning out the (fill in the blank). So, what came first the chicken or the egg? Yes, closets, drawers, cabinets, etc., do need to be cleaned, but you have to choose which job you're going to do first and that's the job you start and then finish.

Sometimes it's hard when cleaning a room to pass by a closet or cabinet that you've been shoving stuff in and closing the door fast so nothing falls out, right? Well, it's going to stay that way for at least a little while longer. Get over it!!

So the eternal question is, "Do I clean the house and then the cabinets, closets, and drawers"? Or do I do the cabinets, drawers, and closets before I tackle the house? Do the house first. At least that much is done and you can stop making excuses to yourself and your company about the dirt. And anyway, as long as you or your company doesn't open any of those cabinet, drawers, and closets; nobody knows. Then there is always the possibility that after you've cleaned the house you are so jazzed with "clean" that the momentum will spur you to greater heights or depths, like those closets.

PREPARATION

Before you do any type of cleaning, *BIG JOB* or maintenance, you need to prepare yourself and the house so you can actually do it and get it done.

First, there is you. Set yourself up to succeed, don't shoot yourself in the foot before you begin. Say to yourself, "Today (or this morning) I'm going to (Fill in the blank)". Dress yourself appropriately; that, my dear, is work clothes. Take off the jewelry and get your nails done tomorrow – after the job. Clean today and get your nails done tomorrow.

Second, turn on the music and turn it up. It needs to be loud enough to hear over the vacuum. Put on something that makes you want to move; something that gets your pulse racing, rock-n-roll, heavy metal, bee bop. Absolutely no classical, no blues, no soft dinner music is to be played while cleaning. Open all the drapes, blinds and shades, or turn on all the lights. You want it light, bright and rockin. All cleaning must be finished by about 3:00pm because after that time the light starts to fade and you don't see the dirt with the same clarity as you did at 10:00am.

Third, methodically, go around the room or rooms and put everything away that isn't where it belongs. If you find you have a lot of stuff that doesn't have a permanent home or you don't like where it is; get a laundry basket, cardboard box, or trash bag and put it in there. Move it out of your line of sight. If you have a two story house and you're cleaning downstairs today; just put everything that belongs upstairs on the stairs until you are finished. Do not make any trips upstairs until you are finished, unless your only potty is upstairs. If you must go upstairs, take something up with you and drop it at the top of the stairs – go potty – and go back down stairs.

Fourth, get all your tools together before you start. Did you get the caddy listed in the tools section? Load it up with all the tools: spray bottles (3), pumice, brushes, scrubby, pull out the vacuum and all its tools, get the rags and now you're good to go.

HOW OFTEN SHOULD YOU CLEAN?

That is a very good question. Some people have a very low threshold for dirt, we call those The Compulsives. They feel they need to clean every day. The other end of the spectrum are people who don't recognize dirt, we call them Men. "What?" "Clean?" "I only just moved in here 3 *years* ago, what's there to clean?"

Maintenance cleaning of some rooms needs to done at least once a week; like the toilet; or more frequently if you have a large number of males living in the house. I still want to know; where do they think all that stuff goes when they shake? The kitchen should be done every day that you cook. Yes, I said every day! Not the whole kitchen, just the parts that were used and abused; like the stove top and counter on either side of the stove, the frig handle, and the sink. The cabinet fronts and floors can wait for a week, maybe. If you make it a habit to clean up after yourself while you're cooking; wipe those grease splatters, or spills on the floor, as soon as it occurs, you can get the dirt off before it dries or hardens.

The *BIG JOB* should be done at least once a year for the average house. If you have young children, animals (especially shedders), or your maintenance schedule is either hit-n-miss or nonexistent; you might consider a BJ twice a year. Let me clarify children; one teenager = 2 children, one retired husband = 1 child, each unemployed child living with you between the ages of 19 and 40 = 2 children.

Cleaning takes discipline; you need to decide just what you want to accomplish and just do it. If you have small children that you can't get rid of, and no, stuffing them in a closet is not an option; then during the time you are cleaning, you need to make them work for you. Give them a job. Give them a rag; give them some simple instructions, like dust all spindles going up the stairs, and let them go. If you show them what you want them to do, they may not do a good job; but they will be occupied, think they are helping, and will just love it.

CLEAN IT UNTIL 'ITS' CLEAN!

No really, I'm serious! The whole idea behind this book is that there is a difference between simply waving a rag over something and "cleaning". When you're cleaning, *you clean it until it comes clean*! If you have to spray and wipe, or spray and mop the same spot more than once to get all the dirt off then that's what you gotta do!

This is most evident when doing floors. High traffic areas may need to be mopped more than once, even if you are doing it every week. You spray and mop until your rag comes up clean. Then you "finish" with vinegar.

In the kitchen, after you "clean" a cabinet door, especially the edges near the handle, touch it – if it is sticky or tacky – it's not clean. Clean is smooth, sleek, slick, and *not tacky to the touch*. Keep spraying and wiping until it "feels" clean. When we do a Spring Clean all the girls have learned how to use the green scrubby on cabinet doors and not do too much damage. If you use the scrubbie "flat handed" you will eventually work through the grease and get down to the cabinet, then "finish" it with vinegar.

If you understand that when you touch something; anything, you leave behind both natural body oil and acid. If you get enough of these two on something that has a varnish type of finish, together they eat the finish. So when you clean all these bodily fluids and dirt off a cabinet door or arm chair, there's a real good chance that the finish is coming off too. Any damage that's done taking the dirt off is not anyone's fault. The oils and acids actually did the damage and you're just seeing the end result. Take off the dirt, oops, off came the finish! Actually the finish has been gone for a while but the dirt just covered it up.

The grit cloth offers the same challenge. This little thing is great getting hard water marks off sinks and sink hardware, but beware you can scratch your fixture to death just as easily. For wood furniture pieces, especially the arms of chairs with generations of body oils, I have used the grit cloth to scrape the oil/acid/grime off.

After you've cleaned your sink or tub and the surface is rough, sandpapery, like a non-skid surface, it's probably scale or mineral deposits. You can see the difference if you know what you're looking for. The area at the base of the faucet is dull and slightly darker than the sink. If you have a dark colored sink it's really obvious! Use the "touch" test; clean the sink; dry it. Now using your index finger move from the outside of the sink toward the hardware (faucet). If it doesn't feel the same, it's not clean. If it does feel the same, you are an exceptional house cleaner and deserve my applause. If you're not sure if it's clean or dirty, you need to give this book to a friend and start looking for someone to clean your house.

MORE "LITTLE" TRICKS!

When doing the *BIG JOB* for the first time, you're probably going to be using KK full strength for most of the job. When I said earlier that a gallon of KK would last a year, that is assuming that your house is 'clean' and you are using it for maintenance. You could, conceivably, use a gallon on the BJ. The KK will do most of the work for you if you let it. When you spray something give it a few seconds to move the dirt. If you wait, you'll see the dirt run down the front. SO spray, count, and then wipe.

When using KK full strength, it is recommended that you then "finish" with vinegar. The KK will do the cleaning but then you need to get all the KK off. When you "finish" something, spray it with vinegar and wipe with a clean MFR. This includes room doors, glass, all kitchen appliances, cabinet doors, porcelain fixtures (toilet, tub, sinks).

After the *BIG JOB* you'll still need to use the KK full strength in a few places in the maintenance phase. This is explained in detail in the Maintenance Chapter.

THE NITTY GRITTY

If you haven't already peeked in the back of this book, there is a section titled The NITTY GRITTY (Hereafter referred to as NG) which include detailed instructions on cleaning individual items; like, ceiling fans, baskets, microwave ovens, blinds, stoves, etc. So rather than burden you with this information while you're trying to get through the book, you can pick and choose what you need to know as it relates to your own particular home.

HOW MANY THINGS DO YOU HAVE IN YOUR HOUSE THAT YOU HAVE NEVER CLEANED EITHER BECAUSE YOU DIDN'T KNOW HOW OR YOU COULDN'T BE BOTHERED?

If you didn't clean it because you didn't know how, now you have no excuse. If you didn't clean it because you couldn't be bothered – you should probably throw it out. I've always wondered, "How dirty does something need to get before it gets cleaned"?

Pop Quiz: Anyone living in your home have allergies or difficulty breathing? getting rid of all that dust and dirt will make a world of difference for breathing problems and it will also improve how your house smells. Not that it smells bad now; but when you're finished, it will actually "smell clean". There will be tons of other uses for vinegar, but I'll address them as they arise.

When doing the big job you'll want to have one bottle each of the KK, KK5/1 and vinegar with you where you are working, the second set outside in the yard for all those things you will be taking out there to clean (more about that later), and a third set in the kitchen, so that's nine you'll need for the big job.

ATTENTION!!! CRITICAL!!! DON'T MISS THIS!!! (No kidding)

PLAN OF ATTACH

This is probably the most important advice I have for you before you attack your first room:

CLEAN THE WORSE THING IN THE ROOM FIRST!!!!!

Seriously, think of doing this job as a day hike. If the first part of the hike is uphill then coming home, when you're tired, is down hill, piece of cake! You don't want to be half way through your hike and be confronted with the worse part of the trip. By the same token you don't want to be 3 hours into the kitchen job and then have to do the worse thing in the room, the range slice. It *will be* murder.

Planning your attack includes deciding what is the dirtiest or hardest thing in the room to clean? In the kitchen, that is the slice that has the range. In the bathroom that is the shower. In "other" space that is probably the ceiling fan or chandelier. If you do the worse thing in the room first, then the rest of the room is a skate. You ***don't*** want to tackle the range slice 2-3 hours into the kitchen BJ. You'll probably never finish, and if you do the results will probably be iffy.

So you can't follow the PATH exactly, no problem, like I said, "every rule has its exceptions", get over it.

Here's the test: if you are going to clean any room and your first thought is "uuggghhh, I've got to clean the XXXXX" (fill in the blank) that's what you want to do first. Nothing else in the room will be as hard as whatever XXXXX was.

CHAPTER 3
The Path

"Follow me my child and I will show you THE PATH."

Jan

the "Head Rag Dragger"

Ladies and gentlemen, boys and girls, and all the ships at sea; may I have your attention please? This is the moment you have all been waiting for. This is where I reveal "THE PATH". (Drum roll please, someone dim the house lights).

The PATH is simple; start at the beginning and end when there is nothing else to clean! Nah! Just kidding.

Seriously, The PATH is exactly that, a PATH. You follow it for both the big job and maintenance. This chapter will describe The PATH doing the BIG JOB. However, for maintenance you still follow The PATH omitting the detail part of the job. Maintenance is just cleaning the big picture, not the detail. So, here it is, "THE PATH":

1. Top to bottom

2. Take it DOWN and Take it OUT (Big Job only)

3. A slice at a time (don't bite off more than you can chew)

4. Back to front

5. Move in ONE DIRECTION – there is no going back!

6. What's in the middle?

7. Finish the floor and you're out!

Now, as with every rule, there will be exceptions and here's the first. The PATH can be strictly adhered to in "OTHER" spaces which are living rooms, dining rooms, bedrooms, den, offices, blah, blah, blah. The exceptions are the nasty rooms, the kitchen and bathrooms.

This chapter will essentially be an overview of The PATH. I will go into serious detail when we actually start cleaning a room in the "BIG JOB" chapters. The NITTY GRITTY will have everything else you need to know.

I have added a page in the back of this book with The PATH so you can tear it out for reference. (Aren't I a sweetie?) There will be no pictures in this chapter. If you absolutely need pictures to understand what I'm describing, you can refer to Chapter 5 or The Nitty Gritty. If I were you, I'd just tough it out without flipping back and forth; it will all become clear by the time you finish the book.

Step #1 - Top to Bottom

Gravity says that anything that falls *will fall down*. Even if you slept through basic science you know this. By starting high in a room, all the dirt will fall down onto those things that you have *not cleaned yet,* so not a problem! Look, it's bad enough doing this job once; you don't want to clean *anything* a second time

Top to bottom means the FIRST thing you do in *any* room (that's *all* rooms, *every* room) is vacuum where the wall meets the ceiling, and all corners where wall meets wall.

Yeah, up there, where no man or woman has gone before! There *are* cooties up there; cob webs, little black flecks (spiders), and that spit ball that went awry. In some sections of the country, like the desert where I live; we have lots of things up there and we should do that at least once a year. In a house with average height ceilings your canister with both poles and the crevice tool will get the job done.

If you are in a house with ceilings above 10-11 feet, you'll probably have to go up a ladder with your canister, poles, and crevice tool to reach the top; or use the Webster. Whatever you use, this job needs to be done first.

If your house has ceiling fans; that is the next thing you do. There is nothing more "at the top of the room" than ceiling fans. (The word ceiling is the clue). You also want to do this early on because of the mess it will make. Details to clean the ceiling fan is in The NG.

Step #2 – Take it Down and Take it Out (Get the ladder out we're going up!)

All the high stuff you have in your house has to come down so it can be cleaned. If you have "stuff" (which is anything other than the actual top of the piece of furniture) on bookcases, cabinets, tall boys, breakfronts, curio cabinets, pot shelves or hanging high on walls in any room; it's coming down. It has probably not been touched (which translates to 'cleaned') since you put it up there when you moved into your house. Not only is it coming down; it's going out!

It's Going Out! This is when most of my customers seize on me. Before you start the actual cleaning of the room; remove as much of this stuff as you can, and take it outside or to the kitchen to be cleaned. If you don't have an "outside" (yard, patio) or the weather is bad (snow, raining) you could use your garage or you'll clean it in the bathroom. I'm talking lots of stuff. Here is a partial list of the big stuff that goes out:

> Venetian blinds (these are a piece of cake to clean anywhere but on the window)
>
> Anything wrought iron that you can move
>
> Silk plants, flowers, trees and their containers
>
> Metal wall hangings and sculptures, sconces
>
> Baskets (all kinds), straw stuff
>
> Large vases, urns, (metal, ceramic, wood)
>
> Stuff from the pot shelves (bowls, vases, birdhouses, cages, etc)
>
> Ceramic pots, bowls, do-dads

Here's a partial list of the small stuff that goes into the kitchen; anything small that is glass, ceramic, or metal from table tops, display shelves, bookcases, etc.

After you remove everything to the outside and/or to the kitchen, the only stuff you should have in the room that you're cleaning is furniture, lamps, rugs, electronic furniture and items to heavy to move like the 7 foot cigar store Indian in the corner.

NOTE: Remember in the list of tools there are 9 spray bottles. Here is why. Three (one each of KK, KK5/1 and vinegar) spray bottles are with you as you clean, three are outside to clean what just went out, and three are in the kitchen to clean the small stuff.

It's going in ....the dryer:

Your clothes dryer is just a big vacuum cleaner that goes round and round. Take all the loose fabric items such as fiber, fabric wall hangings, pillows, valances, drapes, lap rugs; and run them through the dryer on low or no heat for 15-20 minutes with a dryer sheet. When they are done set them aside until the room is cleaned.

Step #3 - A Slice at a Time – *Don't bite off more than you can chew.*

We will be cleaning all rooms in "slices". Walk around and look at your room trying to identify the 'slices'. What you have in a room (furniture, walls, doors) will determine just what makes a "slice". This is shown in detail with photos in Chapter 5 BJ in Other Space.

A slice should be no wider that your arms stretched out from you body or as defined by a piece of furniture or architectural detail, such as a door or window.

If you are consumed with curiosity look at the pictures 5.1 thru 5.4 in Chapter 5 and see what defines slices in the living room I'm cleaning. You need to clean each slice independent to whatever is on either side of it from the top to the bottom, back to front.

Step #4 – Back to Front

This may be obvious, but then again it may not, but I'm going to explain it anyway. Just like the top-down idea, back to front is the same concept, but it is played on a horizontal plane instead of a vertical plane.

Imagine this; look at any wall in your house. It probably has a picture and furniture, like a table, and stuff on the table. The picture on the wall is highest and farthest from you so that is the top back. Immediately below the picture is the table. On the table is stuff and a lamp, and below that is the floor. THAT IS ONE SLICE TOP TO BOTTOM – BACK TO FRONT.

Step #5 – Move in One Direction – *there's no going back!*

Move around the room either from the right or the left but MOVE ONLY IN ONE DIRECTION! I would move to my left because I'm right handed and my cleaning rag is in my right hand. If I'm moving to the left; I won't be crossing in front of my self to clean a slice. Hold a rag in your cleaning hand; if you move in the opposite direction, you will be cleaning *into* the dirt.

Moving in one direction and executing a scorched earth policy in a "slice", that "slice" is totally, completely, and utterly *finished*. The way I explain it to my girls when training is this: "you start here (pointing to the door way) and you go either right or left. If you should happen to drop dead before you have completed the room; while the EMTs are wheeling your body out, I can get a replacement and show her where you started, where you expired, and she can start from there without trying to figure out what is done or needs to be done." They get that!

It's also important to decide how far out from the wall you are going to clean and then be consistent. Walk around your living room and draw an imaginary line around the room on the floor in front of your furniture. This line should be about the same distance from the wall on all 4 walls. So as you clean each slice, you clean up to this imaginary line and what's left is the middle of the room.

Step #6 – Whatever is left in the Middle – *probably more dirt!*

So far we have cleaned our way around the perimeter of the room in slices, top to bottom, back to front. (Think of the perimeter as any piece of furniture that is up against a wall.) After you are finished cleaning everything around the perimenter we are completely and totally finished with that section of the room. There is no going back! Now you move to the middle. Remember we only want to clean anything, everything once! Make sure you clean the middle of the room without disturbing what's already been cleaned!

Do you have sofas, coffee tables, chairs in the room that are not around the perimeter? This is the middle. By separating what is on the perimeter from what is in the middle of the room, you can clean without thinking about the job. Just follow the trail until you get back to where you started. See, I told you; you start here, end here, and you're done.

Step #7 – What's Left of the Floor and You're Ouuuttt!

To clarify "what's left of the floor", remember as we followed The PATH around the room, we pulled out all the furniture and everything else that we could and cleaned behind it and under it so all *that* floor is clean. As you returned each piece and moved to the next slice, you are now totally, completely, and utterly *finished* with that piece of floor.

Since I have no idea what you, the reader, have for floors; I am going to explain floors in The NITTY GRITTY in order to simplify writing the rest of this tutorial. So when I write, "do your floor" you will use one of the three options. And that, my dear, is The PATH!

The simplicity of The PATH is that once you get it down you don't have to think – you just clean. What you have to do now and what you do next is defined. Where you are going – around the room – is a no brainer. Another benefit of following the PATH is you can start and stop a cleaning job as often as necessary. Just go back and start at the next slice! Like I said in the beginning; start here, end here, Voila!!! Fini!!!

CHAPTER 4
The Big Job

When I'm selling the *BIG JOB* to a potential customer, the easiest way to describe it so they understand the scope of the job is, "if you own it and it is in the house we will clean it." But the truth is they still don't understand!

Sounds simple enough to me, but most people don't get it. They almost can't imagine cleaning the whole house. When my company does a BIG JOB, I send a crew of 3 to 7 girls into a house and in 4-5 hours everything in it is cleaned. Everything, including a few things the owner didn't know could be cleaned. The house sparkles, it smells good and all the girls and I go out for a drink and lunch to celebrate another victory over dirt. Us – 1, Dirt – 0!

Of course you won't be able to BJ your whole house in a few hours but you can do a room in a few hours. You can even BJ just one wall in a room if that's all the time you have! After a couple of days your house can sparkle and smell clean too.

That's the beauty of The PATH. When you get the time to restart the BJ you know, without a doubt, what is clean, what still needs to be cleaned and you can easily pick up where you left off.

OK, now a pop quiz: How do you know when something is clean? That answer is simple; *it's clean when it's no longer dirty!* See, I told you the answer was simple.

When I hire a new employee, it takes on the average, two months to fully train them before I'm comfortable that they can do the job the way I want it done. We're talking about women that have cleaned for years; their own house as well as houses for other people. They think they know how to clean. Of course, that changes after their first day with me and The PATH. I have not had one employee who wasn't stunned with the simplicity of The PATH and its effectiveness.

New employees learn The PATH in the BIG JOB first. I give them a tutorial (much shorter than this) and work in the same room with them for the 1st or 2nd job. I check what they have done while they are doing it and usually it's still dirty. "Do it again" I tell them. "But I just cleaned it" they say. "Then why is it still dirty?" I ask as I clean it again and show them the dirt I just took off the thing they just cleaned? "Oh!" they say. There is a difference, a very big difference, between cleaning something (waving a rag over it) and *cleaning it*. There are no degrees of clean. It is either clean or dirty because the middle path is "almost clean" or "not as dirty".

In my directions in the rest of this book, when I say to spray and wipe what I really want is for it (whatever it is) to be sprayed and wiped until it is clean. Some things are easier to clean than others.

Floors around the perimeter of a room that get very little traffic are naturally cleaner than high traffic areas. No duh! So you may have to use several rags and work to clean the high traffic areas. Something that has been hanging on a wall for years (when did you move in?) and only dusted will take more to clean than something that is fairly new and hasn't had the chance to accumulate a 5 year old layer of dirt. When we get into kitchens and bathrooms we've got another whole bag of snakes to deal with.

The BIG JOB ideally should be done at least once a year especially if you have young children, teenagers, husbands, pets or you actually live in your house. So let's say you've lived in your house for 5 years; you have 6 kids, three dogs, two cats and you're not sure about that gerbil and haven't done the BIG JOB yet. My bet is *you need one,* so please finish this book and then do it.

Does anyone living in your house have problems breathing? Asthma? Allergies? Do you or anyone in your house have allergies to dust, dust mites or cooties? Doing the *BIG JOB* will eliminate the majority of the irritants and a good maintenance plan will help keep the place habitable. Believe me when I say "habitable". One of my grandsons has such a ferocious allergy to dust that he is unable to play in the house of his best little friend. This makes him sad, but he will not go into that house because he all but stops breathing after about 10 minutes. That's what I mean about habitable.

Am I scaring you yet? Fear not. You are made of better stuff. You can do this. I believe in you and you and you. I believe with this book you'll do just fine, so let's do it.

The 3 chapters that follow this will be a detailed description of how to 'actually" do the BIG JOB in the three types of rooms. The chapters which are titled "BJ in......." should be read "BIG JOB", not "Barbara Jean" or "Betty Jane" or whatever else you may translate "BJ" to mean.

There will be a few pictures and only enough verbiage to get the idea across. (This really ends up being a lot of verbiage, sorry!)

I'm sure when reading these chapters the first time you'll think this to be an overwhelming task, but it really isn't. OK, maybe it is, but what are you going to do? You're not going to find anyone to do this size job for you and I'm not coming out to your house to do it for you. Just think of the airfare!!! Also, if it's any consolation, the first time you do the BIG JOB, you're going after how many years worth of dirt? After that, if you do this job once a year or 18 months you only have a year's or so worth of dirt, so it really won't be that bad.

On the average, it should take about 4 hours to do each room in your house. No, you didn't read a typo – about 4 hours is what's its going to take; some rooms take a little more some a little less. Trust me the first room will take the longest because you're going to be reading this book while you're trying to clean; tough but doable.

There are a few instances where the only way to get all the dirt off is to take off the finish. This usually happens when doing kitchen cabinets. We've taken off more finish that I'd like to admit, but it is repairable.

You know something is clean (whatever 'it' is) because it's silky, like a baby's bottom. Wipe you hand across the front of any picture with glass, is it silky? Smooth, sleek, silky? No, then it needs to be cleaned. Does all the stuff in your house that is supposed to shine actually shine? No, then it needs to be cleaned. Are your green artificial and silk plants actually green? No, they're dull, with a gray haze on them, then they need to be cleaned. Need I go on?

I'm sure a few have asked yourselves' why are we talking BIG JOB? What about maintenance cleaning? Good question! Maintenance cleaning is *keeping* something clean. As I tell my new customers, without doing the BIG JOB first the only thing we can do is maintain the status quo and that includes all the other dirt that we haven't gotten to yet. Chapter 9 covers maintenance and the path to do maintenance is "The PATH", minus the detail.

OK, LET'S DO DIRT!

CHAPTER 5
BJ in 'Other' Space

In order to maintain the flow and rhythm of the PATH, detailed instructions to clean specific things will be found in The Nitty Gritty. So when we get to these items, refer to The Nitty Gritty for the specifics.

When you enter the front door you are in the foyer, three feet in front of you is the coat closet so if you go left that's the hall to the kitchen and bedrooms; to the right is the living room. Turning right you're standing in the arch facing the living room. Follow the pictures marked Pictures 5.1 through 5.4; that's the living room.

Before you begin; you *are* dressed for the occasion, you have all your equipment and tools with you; the music is on and loud, and the room is light and bright, Right? In the kitchen you need to have your three spray bottles (KK, KK5/1 and vinegar); make sure the sink(s) and the counter(s) on either side are empty. Lay out a few clean MFR on one side of the sink to put the things as you wash, so they can dry while you do the room. The dirty stuff goes on the other side of the sink. (If you are right handed, dirty goes on the left and clean goes on the right, and the sink is in the middle.) If you're able to take things outside to clean, make sure you have a hose and nozzle on the hose and 3 more spray bottles (KK, KK5/1 and vinegar) and hopefully a sunny place for them to dry. If you don't have an outside space to clean your stuff, make room near a bathroom and spread out the shower curtain; lay a few clean cloths

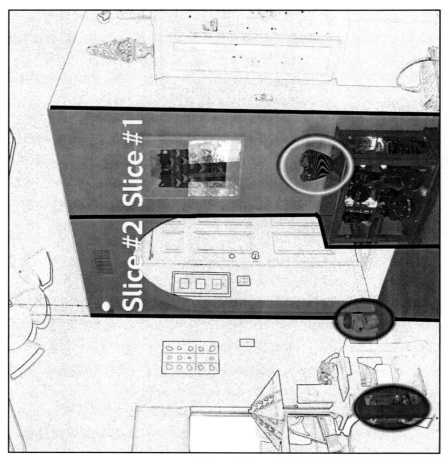

Photo 5.1
Slices 1, 2

down so you can put the clean stuff on to dry. Now follow me on The "PATH"

THE PATH Step #1 "TOP TO BOTTOM"

Put your poles on your vacuum with the crevice tool and vacuum all the way around the room where the wall meets the ceiling and all the corners ceiling to floor then, put the vacuum down. If you do not have the poles for your vacuum or you can't reach the ceiling then this is where you would use the Webster. (This is also where you would be making vacuuming sounds.)

Next is the ceiling fan. You'll notice in Picture 5.3 Slice #7 the fan is hanging over the coffee table. Move the table out of the way and lay the shower curtain on the carpet. (That is the same shower curtain you're going to lay stuff on to dry near the bathroom. Use it here first then put it where you're going to need it later). Put up your ladder and remove the globes; but you'll probably have to remove the bulbs first, then the glass globes. Take the glass to the kitchen; spray with KK and rinse under very hot water and set aside. Go back to the fan. Please read "Fans" in the Nitty Gritty section so you don't break one of the blades off since they cannot be repaired – or you'll end up having to buy a new fan!

THE PATH Step #2 "TAKE IT DOWN – TAKE IT OUT"

Looking at the photos of the room (5.1 to 5.4) I have circled everything that will be removed from the room *before I begin cleaning the room.*

Glass bowl on low display cabinet – kitchen (Slice #1)

Photo 5.2
Slices 3, 4, 5, 6

Snoopy on floor – kitchen (Slice #2)

Bust of David – outside (Slice #3)

Glass w/candle under table – kitchen (Slice #4)

Yellow/blue man on top of curio cabinet – kitchen (Slice #6)

Christmas tree next to curio cabinet – outside (Slice #7)

Baskets under coffee table – outside (Slice #8)

Kitty's cube – outside (Slice #9)

Pillows on chairs – dryer. (Slices #9 & #11)

Go outside and wash what you just took out. Each of the items removed to the outside can easily be cleaned by first spraying liber-ally with vinegar. Use the vinegar like it's free inside, outside and all the little crevices; then rinse with the hose and set off to the side to dry, preferably in the sun, if you have any.

Go into the kitchen and wash everything you took in there. Spray everything with KK and rinse under very hot water, set aside to dry.

NOW go back to the living room because **NOW you're ready to start cleaning the 'room'.**

The PATH Step #3 "A SLICE AT A TIME" (Don't bite off more than you can chew!)

The first 'slice' in this room, moving right to left because I am right-handed, is the slice with the picture and low glass sided display

Photo 5.3
Slices 7, 8, 9

cabinet in Picture 5.1 Slice #1. *"Top to Bottom"* (Step #1) means that you clean the picture first. Remove the picture from the wall and lay flat on the floor. This picture is a piece of original art with glass so you do not want to spray anything on the glass while it is in a vertical position. Lay the picture on the floor and get down there with it and clean the picture (see "Pictures" in NG) rehang picture. To clean the cabinet you need to move it away from the wall far enough to uncover the space that it covers. Now if this piece of furniture is really dirty you may have to vacuum it before you can clean it. Look at the back of the piece – are there dust bunnies hanging off the back? Is there lots of dust around the bottom edge? If there is, suck it up – you don't want to make mud – ugh!!! Now spray the top and all sides of the piece with vinegar and using MFR clean it until it shines (see "Glass" in NG). There is detail at the bottom that may require you use the detail brush to get all the dust out of the detail. If you have to spray the nooks, crannies and ridges a second time and then brush it, then that's what you have to do to get it **CLEAN.** Remember, we are not going into any pieces of furniture so if the inside is dusty and needs to be 'done' that will have to be another day. Now, because this floor is carpeted you have to *edge* (See Floors in NG) where the wall meets the carpet. Using the crevice tool, vacuum where the chest was and then move it back against the wall. If this wall had baseboards you would clean those before you did the floor.

TA DA!!! You just cleaned your first *SLICE* (Step #3) !!!! And you did it *"Top to Bottom"* (Step #1) and *"Back to Front"(Step #4)*! You are absolutely, completely and utterly finished with this slice – so move on – to the left. Oh, and now you're *"Moving in One Direction" (Step #5)*. Now wasn't that easy????? By the time you

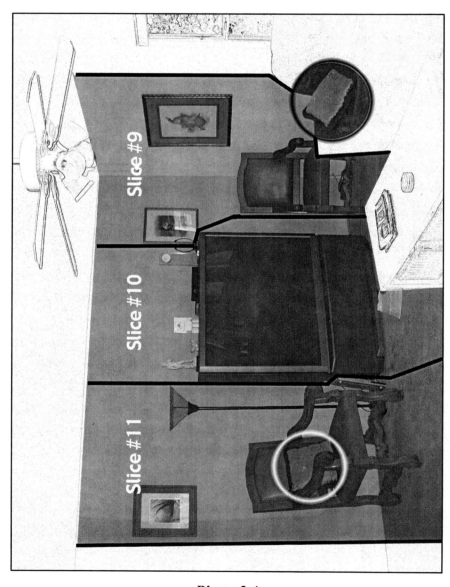

Photo 5.4
Slices 9, 10, 11

finish this room you'll be a pro and then we can go on to the nasty rooms, like the bathroom.

Slice #2 is the archway. Nothing to do in the archway except maybe go for finger prints and dirt. You will find smudges and fingerprints in almost every door way – fact of life – especially if you have children, teenagers, husbands, and occasional visitors. If you have any dirt, spray the dirt with KK and wipe with WTR. KK is dynamite on painted surfaces (literally). Turn the corner (go to Slice #3)

Slice #3 begins when you turn the corner. This wall Photo 5.2 has 4 slices. Slice #3 has a picture and switch plate. Following *"The PATH"*, clean the picture first. Remove it, lay it down, spray, clean and rehang. Spray switch plate and wall around it with KK and wipe with WTR. Edge where the wall meets the carpet, vacuum the carpet out to your imaginary line and move to the left.

Slice #4 is the window and the table. *Back to Front* requires that you do the window first that is in the back of the slice. In order to do this without killing yourself, you need to move any furniture in front of the window out of the way. Unplug the lamp and **put it on the floor behind you** (never move a table with anything on it that can topple over). Also remove anything else on the table and put on the floor too. Ideally, most of what was on the table, except the lamp, went into the kitchen and was washed before you started on the 'room'. Pull the table away from the window far enough to expose the floor it normally covers, out beyond that imaginary line. Pull the window shade up and vacuum the inside of the window to get any cooties, vacuum and then wash the windowsill. Use vacuum to edge where carpet meets wall, vacuum carpet where table stood.

Photo 5.5
Sofa Dumped Over so you can clean behind, and under the sofa.

Turn around and clean table. How dirty is it? If there is a lot of dust around the base and legs, vacuum first. Spray with vinegar; top, legs, bottom shelf and clean with MFR. Use your detail brush to get any old dust and dirt out of the crevices. Put table back where it came from. Now clean the lamp. Remove the shade and immediately put that little thing that holds the shade on back on the lamp so you don't have to go looking for it when you're done. This shade is glass so clean inside and outside with vinegar and MFR. If this were a fabric shade you'd vacuum inside and outside with round brush attachment on canister. Leave lamp on floor and now liberally spray the whole thing with vinegar, bulb and all. Using MFR clean lamp, get the dirt out of any texture, and don't forget to wipe the cord too. Return lamp to table, replace shade and plug in.

The only thing left to do is clean with vinegar anything else that has to go back on the table. Another *slice* cleaned!

Slice #5 and #6 includes the picture over the window and sofa and the cabinet in the corner. *Top to Bottom* requires you clean the picture first; in order to do that you have to move the sofa. Do not drag the sofa forward. You want to dump it forward so that it is upside down (Photo 5.5). This way the floor under the sofa is exposed and you didn't just drag the dirt under it to a new spot. Get on your ladder and remove the picture. Lay it on the floor and clean back, front, and all around. Rehang picture. Next clean the window, just like the last one, edge the wall and while you still have the vacuum in your hand put the upholstery attachment on and vacuum the bottom and back of the sofa. That curio cabinet in Slice #6 is jammed into the corner so before you put the sofa back you're going to have to clean that slice too. Get the ladder and canister with round brush and vacuum the top of the cabinet then spray top with vinegar and wipe it clean. We're not going to move the cabinet because it is full, so we're going to try to vacuum behind it with the canister and at least one pole and crevice tool. There could be cooties on the back of the piece if it has been here long enough. Lightly spray a MFR with vinegar and wipe the back as best you can without toppling the piece. Now edge the floor around the piece as well as where the carpet meets the wall. Now vacuum the carpet and push the sofa upright. If the sofa cushions are removable take them off, vacuum the inside of the sofa, all the cushions top, bottom, all around, and replace. Another 2 slices are done! We're ready to turn the corner.

Picture 5.3 shows 3 slices. (Remember the Christmas tree went outside.)

Slice # 7 starts by removing everything from the table to the floor behind you, and then pulling the end table out far enough so you can get to the picture. Clean the picture. There is also a receptacle on that wall – so clean that, now edge at the wall and vacuum the carpet. Turn around to the table, clean that, then the lamp, then anything else that was on it and push back into place. Move left.

Slice #8 is the sofa/windows. The sofa slice is wide but you don't have a choice. Dump the sofa forward turning it upside down; take stained glass down and wash with vinegar and MFR, vacuum the inside of the window casings. Edge carpet, turn around and vacuum back and bottom of sofa. Vacuum carpet and push sofa back into place. Vacuum sofa cushions – keep on moving on.

Slice # 9 you will find in Photo 5.3 and 5.4; I will be combining the last slice of Photo 5.3 with the first slice of Photo 5.4 and call it Slice #9 because of the way that chair is in the corner. Pull the chair out of corner and clean both pictures, edge the carpet, vacuum the floor, turn and clean the chair. The chair is wood and leather with lots of carved detail. Spray the wood with vinegar and use the detail brush to get all the dirt out of the carving, then wipe dry with MFR, don't forget the back of the chair. Spray a clean MFR lightly with vinegar and wipe the leather. Make sure you get in where the leather meets the wood, that's where the dust accumulates. Edge along the wall, vacuum the carpet, then put the chair back where it belongs.

Slice #10 is the television. Remove whatever is on the top to the floor behind you. Pull out the unit and clean the back and sides, edge the carpet, vacuum the floor, and push unit back. Spray rest of unit with vinegar and wipe clean. Turn around and clean everything that you took off the unit as you are returning it.

Slice #11 – do the lamp first, unplug and pull it out into the room. If you tilt the lamp down and look into the shade you probably have a very interesting collection of bugs and stuff in there. Vacuum out whatever is in there, spray inside of shade and bulb with vinegar, use MFR and wipe clean, spray outside of shade, pole, base, and wipe clean. Pull chair away from wall, clean picture, edge, vacuum rug, turn around and clean chair. Put chair back.

The PATH Step #6 – WHAT'S LEFT IN THE MIDDLE?

We've just cleaned the slices on the 4 walls and the only thing left is what's in the middle of the room which is the coffee table in picture 5.3 Slice #7, and the floor that was not cleaned while we were doing the slices. Remember the imaginary line we were cleaning up to? Clean the table top, bottom, legs, and all around with vinegar and MFR. Vacuum carpet where the table goes, then return table to its spot in the carpet.

THE PATH Step #7 –FINISH THE FLOOR AND YOU'RE OUT!!!

But before you do that go outside and into the kitchen and collect all the stuff you removed before you started cleaning and return it to where it belongs. Pick up all your rags, equipment, tools, ladder, and remove these from the room. Starting at the corner which is Slice #9 move backwards (in one direction) vacuuming towards the archway where you started. Voila!!!! You have just cleaned a room using The "PATH".

NOTE: For those of you that are left-handed you may be more comfortable moving to your right around a room. To do this, start at Slice #11 and move to your right ending at Slice #1.

Now, about that plastic pitcher you purchased, go mix yourself a batch of something yummy and give yourself a well deserved pat on the back, that is, if you can lift your arm that high.

CHAPTER 6
BJ in the Bathroom

The bathroom may very well make or break your resolve to really clean your house. It's a toss up which is the worse room - the bathroom or kitchen – I'll clean a kitchen in a heart beat. The bathroom, well, I'll pull rank first – see I'm the boss – so I always get to do the kitchen.

Now a clean bathroom is truly a thing of beauty. You do this room right and you've got something to be really proud of.

WHAT KIND OF BATHROOM DO YOU HAVE?

There are 3 types of bathrooms. The cozy type: only one person at a time. The roomy bathroom: can accommodate two people, sort of, but never three. And the humongous bathroom which will easily accommodate a dinner party of six with dancing.

Because you can't do anything about the layout of the room, you're pretty much stuck with what you got. So here is where some exceptions to The PATH happen. But trust me it still works. At the end of this book will be a fairly extensive section, The Nitty Gritty has pictures and instructions on how to clean some of the things you're going to have to deal with. So if while reading this you feel the instructions are a bit sketchy look in the back for further detailed instructions.

Something to consider: In any of the bathroom types, you will want to do the sink or at least one sink last. If not, and you have to use the sink, you're going to have to finish it a second time. You don't want to have to do that. So, before you begin, think about your PATH and work toward the sink closest to the door.

THE COZY BATHROOM

This is everything in one room the toilet, sink, tub/shower with just barely enough room to turn around. Remember the rules of The PATH– and the exceptions. All the rules apply but are rearranged slightly to accommodate the space we are cleaning.

It's going out: remove everything except what is attached to the floor or imbedded in the wall. Whatever can be washed outside or in the kitchen, do it now and leave it to dry. We're talking baskets, floral arrangement, shelves, and stuff. Everything else is set outside the room on the floor and includes the roll of toilet paper that's hanging off the side of the vanity. "Everything else" – includes towels, rugs, (maybe you want to wash them now) toothbrush, tissue box, make-up, hair brush, dryer, blah, blah, blah, get my drift?

Top to bottom: Of course you have remembered to vacuum where the ceiling meets the wall first. Then if you have a ceiling mounted exhaust fan and the grill is fuzzy, you need to clean this next. Also any ceiling mounted lighting fixtures (NG). To clean the fan, turn it on and brush the grill with the white utility brush. The fuzzies will be sucked up into the fan, but the grill will be clean. If the exhaust unit has a light, pull the lens of the light down and clean the glass and replace (NG). Now while you have the vacuum in your hands vacuum the baseboards and around the edge of the room – get all that hair and lint/dust up before you spray anything. Don't want to make hairy mud. UGH!!!

Back to front: Standing in the door of the bathroom, the farthest thing from you is probably the tub/shower, if it's not, start there anyway. Remember to do the worse thing first, so that's where you start. Depending on how the tub/shower space is finished you can have any variety of materials in this space or a combination of materials: paint, tile, wallpaper, fiberglass, glass; in addition to shower curtain, sliding door(s) or nothing.

If you have a shower curtain, take it down. If the liner is over 1 year old, toss it, and hang up a new one to commemorate the JOB! If your tub/shower wall does not go to the ceiling and the rest of the wall to the ceiling is finished in another material, look closely at this area. You're going to have to clean this before you start the lower part. With good light, look at the wall and ceiling above the shower enclosure you will probably see brownish spots – This has to go. This is what condensation does when it dries on a not too clean wall. Spray the ceiling and top section of wall with KK and wipe with WT rag. Spray a second time with vinegar and MF rag.

Now spray all the shower walls and hardware with KK. I hope you're dressed for this job because you should be standing inside the tub/shower shoeless and your pants rolled up.

Moving in one Direction: Pick an edge and start scrubbing the shower using the green scrubby. **Remember you're moving top to bottom, in slices, in one direction.** You may have to respray an area several times to get the desired result, which is smooth, silky clean. While scrubbing with one hand you are feeling the surface with the other hand. You'll feel the clean just like you'll feel the dirt. (This is why I can't wear gloves while cleaning – you gotta be able to *feel* the dirt) Use the pitcher to rinse each section as you clean it. Work your way around the tub/shower wall not forgetting the hardware, faucet, knobs, and overflow cover. Also don't forget the top edge of the tile, this is called bullnose tile. You may need a step stool to see this and get it clean (Do this first). When you think you have it clean, run you bare hand over all the walls, if you missed something you'll feel it – re-clean it. **Clean it until it's clean**! Now you need to turn around and do the door(s) if you have them; glass or plastic, you do them the same as the wall. Spray, scrub, rinse, **feel for the clean.** When the walls and doors are clean you need to do the actual tub or shower floor. Hopefully, you thought to step out of the tub to do this. Same PATH, same method; spray, scrub, rinse, feel. If you have sliding shower doors, you need to clean the thing overhead that they hang from and the track they run in. Don't forget the outside of the tub. When it's all clean, you can finish with vinegar and MFR.

Moving on to the next piece in the room; which should be the toilet; if it is not, do it next anyway. (You want your PATH to end at the sink.) Start at the top of the wall above the toilet working down cleaning everything in your path. When you get to the toilet squeeze some SS/b into the bowl and clean it with your toilet brush and put the seat and lid down and let it sit. Spray the rest of the outside of the toilet, the seat, lid, hinges, and the walls surrounding it with KK. Don't forget the wall under the tank and the water lines from the wall into the toilet, especially if you have men in your house.

Did you remove the roll of toilet paper and the holder? Starting at the top of the tank, start cleaning, using your detail brush where necessary. Don't forget the seat/lid hinges. Clean the wall under/

behind the tank and the hardware coming out of the wall to the tank at the floor. Use the detail brush on the top edge of the baseboards and where the baseboard meets the floor using WT rags. If the entire outside is clean flush the toilet and make sure the inside is clean. Feel the inside of the bowl. If it is not completely smooth and slick you have mineral deposits that need to be removed using the pumice stone. Use a flat side of the stone doing small sections at a time moving around the inside of the bowl. You can feel what is clean and what still needs work. You may have to flush the toilet a few times if you want to work in clear water (I do).

Now do the floor on either side of the toilet out to the front so you will be finished with this slice when you move on.

The next piece should be the sink, correct? Wrong – turn around there's probably a wall behind you. Move back to the back of the room and clean moving toward the door cleaning everything in your path ceiling to floor. Make sure you do any corners while on your knees so when you mop the floor on the way out this is done and you won't have to do it then. Why get down on your knees a second time if you don't have to?

Now you can do the sink slice. Top to bottom means you clean the light fixture first, the mirror, then the vanity/sink base. If you have a medicine cabinet in this area, usually on the wall to the side, do this before you finish the sink; remember gravity. The medicine cabinet probably has a thin edge at the top that you didn't even know was there. You need to clean this too. Finish everything with vinegar and MF rags. If your sink has exposed plumbing make sure you clean the wall under the sink behind the pipes, and the pipes down to the floor, then the floor.

Now you can do the sink! Scrub with SS/B and the scrubbie, don't forget to get all the scum off the hardware. Finish with vinegar.

Close yourself in the bathroom (if you have a door) and spray the inside of the door and the jamb with KK and wipe with WT rag. Use your detail brush in any corners and don't forget the edge of the door where that little thingy that latches it is.

Open door and clean the outside of the door the same, finish with vinegar.

Now we get to put everything back. Go find everything you took outside or into the kitchen; make sure it has dried and put it back where it came from. Now everything outside the room on the floor needs to be returned but you need to clean it first. Yep – clean it! Nothing should go back into that room that does not sparkle like it was brand new; and if it doesn't sparkle, you'll notice it every time you go in there. Don't forget to put that toilet paper roll back and hang your new shower curtain and clean towels.

Well, you did it again! I knew you could do it! Now mix your self something refreshing and hopefully numbing and relax and heaven help the first person that messes that room up. I can hear you now!

THE ROOMY BATHROOM

The roomy bathroom typically has a double vanity and the toilet and shower are in a room of its own. If you have two rooms you clean each one separately following The PATH. Do the room farthest from you first following The PATH as explained in the cozy bathroom. Remove everything, start at the top working down, start at the back working forward. If you have to take it outside or into the kitchen to clean it, do that first. When everything is clean and finished replace everything you removed, hang clean towels and close the door. Do not go into this room again until you have finished the second room. If you have to use the potty before you're finished use another one if you have it.

In The Nitty Gritty there are plenty of pictures for cleaning several of the light fixtures you'll find in typical bathrooms. If you don't see something that is similar to what you have, remember this: Take as much of it apart as you can – clean it – and then reassemble it.

THE HUMONGOUS BATHROOM

I've cleaned enough humongous bathrooms to admit that even I can be intimidated. These usually have a garden tub big enough for a foursome, plus a shower. The toilet is in a separate room. And the vanity 15 to 20 feet of countertop, with 2 sinks and too much space to spread out too much stuff.

Before you begin you have to lay out your plan of attack. Remember to do the worse thing first and this is usually the shower. This will probably disrupt the flow of *moving in one direction*, but this is one of those exceptions. After the shower, I'd do the tub and then toilet, and leave the vanity/sinks for last.

To begin, remove everything that isn't nailed down or imbedded in the wall. Empty the place. Now begin cleaning in this order: Shower, tub, toilet, closet floor, and doors, lights/mirror/vanity/sink. Replace everything, then do the floor and you're out!

Do you have a walk-in closet? You're not in here to, "fix" the closet - you can do that another day. Do the lights, any baseboards, doors/jambs, and vacuum (or mop) the floor.

Another job well done!

If you are cleaning one room per day because that is all you have time for – good for you – you'll get to the end soon. But now you have to finish the job. You need to wash your rags WTR and MFR separately, put all you tools away and put your feet up unless it' s time to do dinner in which case you can put your feet up later.

CHAPTER 7
BJ in the Kitchen

I don't have to explain to you that this title refers to the BIG JOB in the kitchen. Well, I hope that is what you read, because that's what I meant.

The kitchen is a whole other beast. Most of the girls that work for me have very definitive opinions about kitchens. They either like them or they absolutely hate them. There is no doubt about how each feels about this room. I, personally, would clean a kitchen over any other room in the house. Ok, I'm sick, but that doesn't make me less lovable.

First fill the sink with hot, hot, hot water and a big shot of KK. This is for soaking stove parts, microwave parts and all those smaller things that clutter your counters. If you have any big stuff, that has to go out (or in the bathroom) to get cleaned, do it now. Everything in this room will be greasy dirty and will need work to get clean. Remember clean it until it's clean!

Following The PATH we're going to start at the top of the room, at the ceiling. If your kitchen cabinets go up to the ceiling (no space) skip this next section.

If your cabinets *do not* go all the way up to the ceiling, you must clean this space first. Get your ladder and go up and remove everything from the tops of all cabinets. When I do this, I start at one end of the counter and walk on the counter to take each piece down and put it on the counter and move to the next item. Do not get down from the counter until you have reached the end. Clean everything you just took down now and leave it to dry. Chances are very good that you will need to KK everything that was up there because they are going to be very greasy. Now, go back and clean the top of the cabinet and don't forget to wipe the wall and ceiling. If it has been a while since you cleaned the tops of your kitchen cabinets you may have some work ahead of you. When there is enough greasy dirt up there you have to work through the layers which means you spray, let it soak, wipe, spray, let it soak, wipe, each time use a clean WTR.

If you want to make the job a lot easier in the future; before you put everything back - cover the tops of the cabinets with newspaper or paper towel– a single sheet will do. When you go up there again, next year (I hope), you may have to clean the stuff that you have up there, but the cabinet tops will be clean – you just throw out the paper and put down new!

Also, check to see if any food has splashed on the ceiling. If there is, you can get it now.

LOOK UP! - does your kitchen have a ceiling fan or hanging light fixture? Make sure you do this early. Can you take the fixture apart? Remove the bulbs, any glass, wash everything and reassemble. Yes, the chain is part of the fixture!

THE STOVE

Remember: **Do the worse thing in a room first** – that will be the stove slice. Prepping the stove slice requires you to remove all parts of the range hood or microwave (see NG) and leave them to soak in the sink filled with hot water and a big shot of KK. Working from top to bottom, you now clean the cabinet over the range hood or microwave, the microwave (inside, outside and bottom), the wall under the microwave, then the stove. After this slice is cleaned, pull the stove away from the wall and clean the sides (dinner for 3 anyone?). Before you spray anything I'd suggest you vacuum all that stuff off the floor. Don't forget the sides of the cabinets that the stove is wedged between. Remove the drawer under the oven, empty it, clean it out, clean the floor under the range, push the range back into place.

Note: I'd be willing to bet that you wouldn't leave a chunk of food out on your stove or counters to slowly dry out, rot, and become a permanent part of the counter. But that's exactly what's happening down the sides of your range unit. While you're cooking food; particles, juices, and grease are dribbling down the sides through that tiny space between the range and the counter. When you finally pull it out you'll see what I mean. All this food stuff is rotten, if it is really greasy, it's probably rancid. If you have any tiny critters living in your house, they would be well fed.

Now, you can start your slices. You can follow the standard PATH moving in one direction cleaning everything in your path. When you get to the refrigerator, pull it out, and clean all 5 sides (top and 4 sides), clean the walls behind and around it, vac/mop the floor under it, and push it back. If your refrig has a grill on the bottom, pull the grill off and wash it. Don't forget to vacuum the space behind the grill. If you have an older refrig, that space is full of coils. These need to be cleaned and should be kept clean on a regular basis since the dirtier they are the harder it is for your refrig to keep its temperature and will have to use lots more electricity to do the same job.

When you're doing a SLICE of cabinet look up under the top cabinet; has anything splashed up there? Does it need to be cleaned? Don't forget, when moving down, to do the **wall under the cabinets**. Just continue to work your way around the room. When you get to the stove, which is already clean, skip over it and keep on moving. You should finish at the sink.

COUNTER TOPS: These are not the easiest things to CLEAN. You think it *looks* clean, but is it? After you think you have cleaned your counter; dry it, and wipe it again with a clean, dry MFR. Just gently wipe the rag over the surface. If you happen onto a dirty (greasy) spot your rag will drag – not glide – over the surface. "But it *looks* clean", you say. "Well, it's not!", I say. This most frequently happens on either side of the range and in the corner under the cabinets that you don't use a lot. To clean the spots, sometimes quite large, spray liberally with KK and scrub with a scrubbie flat handed, using circular motion, no need to press, you're just going to have to work through the dirt. If the color of the counter is light enough you'll see the KK darken. If you have any doubt that you're getting any dirt (grease) up, wipe it with a clean, dry WTR. What did you wipe up? Do the test again. Wipe again. Keep spraying, scrubbing and testing until the rag glides across the entire counter without a hitch. Now it's clean! Finish with vinegar. Oh, don't forget the front edge of the counter, especially on either side of the range. Surprise!! (This is why in the NG under Range - that I recommend you spray both sides of the counter nearest the range every night after you finish dinner. Keep on top of it and you won't spend a half-hour cleaning it during the BJ.)

STUFF ON THE COUNTER: Let's chat a minute about the 'stuff' you put on your counters for decoration. Hey, some of the 'stuff' I've seen is quite nice, even pretty if you can see through the dirt and grease. Don't display it for any reason unless you intend to keep it clean. The benefit (how it looks) demands an investment (keeping it clean).

If you're too busy to maintain something properly you're not doing anything for the ambiance if its slimy. This is where the 'minimalist' decorating idea comes from. Actually, it's because of people like me, who are too lazy or won't make the time to clean it, that minimalism is such a good way to go.

Before I buy something I ask myself, "self, how many times are you going to clean this thing before it gets pitched out the window?" If I can't answer with a triple digit number, I don't buy it. Hey, I've got enough to do just keeping what I have now clean without adding to the job. I also save a lot of money that way – enough to pay someone to clean my house (see, there is a method to my madness (or cheapness).

Before you do the sink make sure you have "finished" all the appliances with vinegar – go for the shine.

Don't forget to put all your stuff back up on the top of the cabinets.

Clean (scrub) the sink and finish it; which means dry it and polish the hardware. Cleaning the sink could take some serious work. First rinse out any goobers, then give it a good healthy squirt of SS/B and scrub with the green scrubby, then rinse. If the sink is heavily stained, recoat with the SS/B and leave it for a while to bleach out the stains, then rinse. While you're waiting for the SS/B to bleach the sink, go "finish" the stove/MWO. Finish the sink; then the last thing you do is the floor and You're OUT!!

The kitchen floor is probably the dirtiest in the house and so it needs extra attention. You have already cleaned under the stove and refrigerator, so that much is done. So how's your kick plate? What is a kick plate you ask????? It is the unsung hero that holds your kitchen counters up. Get down on your knees and notice how the base of the cabinets is indented. This allows you to get close to the counter; this is where you put your feet. When was the last time you cleaned this part intentionally? Now when you were doing your slices if you cleaned your slice down to the floor you should have cleaned this kick plate and used your detail brush to get into the corners and get any of that gunky stuff that has tried to become a permanent part of your floor. If you didn't do this with your slice, you have to do it before you do the floor. But wait there's more…. Return everything to its proper place before doing the floor. You don't want to walk across it a dozen times after it's been cleaned, now do you???

NOW The floor! – If it has been a while since you really, really cleaned your floor, you may have to go over it a few times. Remember to **clean it until it is clean** using KK and WTRs and the swiffer mop. Keep spraying and mopping, changing your rag frequently, until the rag comes up clean. When it's clean, you "finish" it with vinegar.

The last thing I tell my customers after we've finished the kitchen BJ is that they can't cook in there for at least 2 weeks so the clean "takes". So that means you'll have to go out to dinner.

CHAPTER 8
The Group Hug

So what's the GROUP HUG you ask? And what's that got to do with getting my house clean?

Another very good question. You're really a very astute bunch of students. The group hug is a way to get the job done quickly, and in one fell swoop.

After reading this book you realize that to do a BJ (that's Big Job) on your house alone will take weeks, maybe even months depending on how much real time you have to actually dedicate 3 to 4 hours to clean each room just once. Now, when I send my crew into a house to do a BJ, I send in enough girls so that we can be done and out in around 4 hours; we start at 8:00am and we're doing lunch by noon. So, if my estimate to clean a house is 12 man hours, I'll send in 3 girls. 3 girls times 4 hours each equals 12 man hours. The same if the house is BIG, DIRTY or has lots of STUFF. A 24 hour clean will require 6 girls and we'll still be out by noon. (6 x 4 = 24).

So here's how you can do it too. Buy, give or read a copy of this book to your nearest and dearest 4, 5, or 6 friends. Make a pact that together each of you will get together to clean one of your houses in a day (4 hours) and then you all get clean houses and it's only taken you 4 hours per house.

Now, you remember that plastic pitcher that we used to rinse shower walls? Well, you each now have your own pitcher to mix a batch of whatever floats your boat to enjoy together as you enjoy the clean.

Look at the beauty of the idea! In around 4 hours +/- your whole house will be cleaned, scrubbed, shiny and sparkly, and smell good. In the time between when you drop the kids off to school and pick them up, you can do something that you never dreamed could/would happen. Hey, I'll drink to that!

Going one step further, what would happen if you all, as a group, go out and do this for other people, for money? Perfect the job on your own collective houses and then sell your service. There will always be dirt and there will always be people who don't want to clean, can't clean, don't have the time to clean, or would just be glad to pay someone to do it for them.

Now, the idea of cleaning your WHOLE house shouldn't be so daunting. Even if you're a working mom you'd only have to give up a few Saturday or Sunday mornings to accomplish the same thing. Of course, you have to give up some time to the preparation. You'd have to pick up your house, that may be a chore in and of it self, but in the end it would be worth it. Wouldn't it?

Read this book again with a bunch of your friends, use those pitchers now, you have to break them in some time and make a plan. Then make it happen!!

Happy cleaning and enjoy the sparkle!

Love,
Jan
the "Head Rag Dragger"

CHAPTER 9

Maintenance

MAINTAINING A CLEAN KITCHEN

Keeping a kitchen clean is not that difficult once you develop some new habits. I know I sound like your mother. Hey, I sound like *my* mother. But, she was right. When you're not looking, late at night when everyone in the house is sleeping, any greasy dirt in your kitchen that wasn't cleaned up will metamorphose into cement. Oh, you won't notice this happening until you try to clean it weeks later. Trust me, would I lie? Really, it does happen that way. So as to not anger the clean gremlins – get the stuff while it's still new, soft and removable.

KITCHEN - DAILY

If you have a dishwasher there is no reason to put anything dirty anywhere but in the dishwasher. No excuses, no exceptions. Run it every night after dinner and put the clean stuff away either before you go to bed or first thing in the morning.

If you don't have a dishwasher, buy yourself a small plastic tub and put it in the sink or right next to it and ALL the dirty stuff goes in there. Wash everything when it fills up, or at the end of the day and immediately dry everything and put it away. Voila!!! Fini!!!

Here is where those other spray bottles and rags come in. Under your sinks (kitchen and bathrooms) you need to have 3 spray bottles one each of KK, KK5:1 and Vinegar and a stack of about 10 each WTR and MFR.

After the dishes are loaded into the dishwasher and all foods are put away spray your range, microwave front or exhaust hood, refrigerator handles and counters with KK. Now use your WTRs to wipe everything down. While cooking did you get any goobers on your cabinet doors or handles? If you want it to shine; spray and wipe again with vinegar. Throw your rags in the dirty clothes; turn out the light and you're done!

If you have stainless appliances you can use rubbing alcohol to clean it. It's a lot cheaper than most of the cleaners/polishes that are sold for maintaining stainless surfaces. You can use MFRs if it's not too dirty, otherwise use WTRs. Always wipe with the 'grain' of the appliance. If you have something nasty that has dribbled down the front of the appliance use the KK, get it clean, and then finish with the alcohol.

Which KK to use - the full strength or the KK5:1? What did you cook? Did you just microwave something or did you fry up a batch of catfish and okra? How dirty is the range? Just fried up a dinner? I'd drench the whole range and the counter on either side with KK 100% then wipe dry.

KITCHEN - WEEKLY

If you have either an exhaust hood, or a microwave, over your range you have filters underneath that should be cleaned with some regularity. Oh, you didn't know? Yes, those screens come out and should be cleaned. On Saturday night pull the knobs off the stove, take out those filters, take any parts to the range top that are removable and any other knick-knacks on your counters, like those containers that hold your cooking tools and put them in the dishwasher, run it and go to bed. When you get up the next morning it will all be clean and you just have to thank the clean gremlins, put it back, and you're done.

Mop your floors at least once a week if not more frequently depending on the patterns of the inhabitants. Keep your floor swiffer handy and loaded (with a clean rag) to mop any 'accidents'. Don't forget you've got your ammo ready under the sink if you need it between cleanings. Keep replenishing your rags as you use them so there is no reason not to "take care of it" when it happens. You also want to check out your cabinets and handles. Spray a WTR with KK5:1 and wipe the corners and handles. Look for the dirt and get it while it's still new. Old kitchen dirt wants to turn to rock and never come off. Removing new dirt is easy!

KITCHEN - MONTHLY

There aren't too many things to do on a monthly basis if you are keeping the place clean following the daily and weekly suggestions above. But that is really a function of your personal tolerance for dirt.

If you have any critters that are shedders; cats, long haired dogs, dogs that blow their coat; you want to remember to clean the bottom vent and coils on the refrigerator. Pull the vent, wash it, and vacuum the coils.

KITCHEN - ANNUAL

Once you get the kitchen clean, and you are maintaining it on a regular basis, you only need a BJ once a year - in this room anyway.

Because of the nature of the grease that gets into the air from cooking, you can bet the tops of your cabinets will need to be cleaned again a year from now. Do you have to pull your stove and refrigerator? I don't know, has any cooking slime migrated down the side of the range? Remember though, the more you stay on top of the nasty dirt, the easier it is to keep your home clean. Grease is the biggie. If you let grease dry, it hardens and then you have to blast it off.

BATHROOMS

There really isn't any good "schedule" for cleaning a bathroom, especially one that is used every day. It also comes down to your personal threshold for dirt. If you feel like you're always apologizing to your guests for the condition of the bathroom then you probably need to increase the frequency of "cleaning".

Here's what you've got: hair, skin, hair spray, towel lint, powder, make-up, perfume, toilet paper lint and then you have your regular dust. If you have men you have overspray (you know what I mean). And all this stuff is ALL over the room.

If you didn't know it, soap scum is actually grease scum. Bar soap uses grease as its base. Look up the original receipt for soap that our ancestors made; its fat, ash and some other stuff. So go after soap scum with a degreaser – which is – Taa Daa – KK. If you use liquid body wash in the shower you don't have as much of a problem. Also use KK in the bathroom sinks. "Finish" both with vinegar for a shiny clean surface.

Do you have an exhaust fan in the ceiling of the room? Look up, is the grill fuzzy? Well if it is, that same fuzz is all over the room.

A good cleaning once a year works for some; every six months is a better idea if there is more than one person using this room on a regular basis.

In Chapter 1 where I told you get 9 spray bottles; after the BJ is done, three of them go in this room under the sink, one each of KK, KK5/1 and Vinegar plus a stack of about 10 each WTR and MFR. If you have mineral deposits in your toilet you also want to keep a pumice stone handy and a bottle of SS/B.

BATHROOMS - DAILY

Think of prevention as your friend. When you are finished taking your shower either squeegee or wipe down the walls and shower doors. When you brush your teeth rinse the sink of any of those nasty globs of toothpaste before they turn to stone.

Always, before cleaning a bathroom, get your canister out and vacuum up all the hair, powder and lint before you start cleaning. Powder turns to glue if you wet it – don't want to do that! Like with the BJ: start at the top and work down. And the top should include the light bulbs over the sink especially if you use hairspray. Dust them and if they don't look clean they're not! You probably need to wash them – weekly if that's what it takes to keep them clean! Pssst – let the bulbs cool before you spray them; just a friendly note.

Do you have a toilet brush next to the toilet? Every toilet should have its own brush and it should be used frequently.

When you think about it, a clean bathroom even "smells" better.

Here's a trade off: if you spent your apologizing time tidying up the bathroom you'd be at a draw.

BATHROOMS - MONTHLY/ANNUAL

You shouldn't have much to do on a monthly basis if you are cleaning up your messes as you make them. If you're not cleaning up after yourself you probably need to do a BJ every month.

OTHER SPACE

The biggest challenge with keeping Other Space clean is keeping it picked up.

Rule #1: Do not lay anything down.

Rule#2: Put it where it belongs.

When all else fails.....

Rule #3: Chuck it!

You know the old saying: A place for everything and everything in its place. It really works. **If something doesn't "have a place" make one or throw it out.** There are tons of charitable organizations that would love to have what you are tired of. By the way, my middle name is Chuck (it), just ask my family. The problem could simply be that you have more STUFF than you have places for. If this is the case you either have to *move to a bigger place* or *get rid* of the STUFF! We all know you can't put 10 pounds of STUFF in a 5 pound bag. Oh, I know, you're trying to.

When cleaning Other Space on a maintenance plan you basically follow The PATH just not with the same *attention to detail*. Here it is:

Step #1 - Top to bottom

Step #3 - One slice at a time

Step #4 - Back to front

Step #5 - Move in one direction

Step #6 - Do the middle

Step #7 - Do the floor and you're out!

Did you notice that I omitted Step #2? We're not taking anything down or out and we're not going to move furniture unless we absolutely have to.

To start the maintenance in any room, first get your tools together. Caddy with 3 spray bottles (KK, KK5/1, and vinegar), vacuum(s), swiffer mop, swifter duster, WTR and MFR. Turn on the lights and turn up the music (except if the baby is sleeping, and then put in your ear buds).

The swiffer duster is allowed in the maintenance routine. Use this to reach anything that you cannot get to without moving furniture or going up on a ladder. Do you have pictures on the wall behind the sofa? If you can stand on the sofa do it and dust it with a rag, if you can't, won't, or would rather not stand on the sofa, use the swiffer to dust the frame and glass. Definitely use the swiffer to do the blades of the ceiling fans. If you have hanging ceiling lights, whack the chain and top of the fixture.

You picked up the room, right? Everything is "in its place". Now pick a starting place, preferably the door way to the room and start from there. Remember The PATH when we did the BJ in the living room. Why not do your maintenance following that same PATH. Don't reinvent the wheel if you don't have to.

Get a MFR and spray both sides lightly with vinegar and go for it. Dust everything in each slice from top to bottom. Picture frames, glass on picture, lamp, everything on the table, then the table to the floor. If your MFR gets dry, spray it again. If it is dirty, throw it behind you and get another one. Go all the way around the room. Pick up all the dirty rags that you've thrown down, vacuum, mop and you're out.

On the average, maintenance cleaning in Other Space rooms shouldn't take more than 20 to 30 minutes to do. This, of course, is based on you doing some maintenance cleaning at least once per month and you have had a BJ in the last year.

However, if you have shedders (cats and dogs), or screamers (small children) and teenagers; you might want to do your maintenance weekly. So, a 7 room house should take just over three hours per week. Do a room a day if that's all the time you have, that's a ½ hour per day for maintenance.

Vacuuming and mopping can be a challenge since we want to move as little furniture as possible to get the job done. This is where the canister/upright combination or an upright with all the attachments offers the best option. If, because of its size, you can only vacuum the middle of your room and not get under any furniture, you should have a canister. There usually is a floor attachment that comes with the vacuum; however most of these are designed to be used only on hard floors (tile, pergo, linoleum, wood) only. I have an Oreck that has an attachment that can be used on carpet/rugs and hard floors. This way you can vacuum under chairs, tables; any piece of furniture with enough clearance to get under it without moving it. If this isn't an option for you, you're going to have to move some of your furniture to get under it.

Does this plan sound too simple? Now you do understand that this maintenance plan is based on the house having been BJ'd already. Since everything is really *clean,* just dusting with a rag lightly sprayed with vinegar *will* do the job. Like I said earlier, you can only dust for so long then you have to *clean it*!

CHAPTER 10
The Nitty Gritty

This section will give detailed instructions how to clean various things in your house. I've put them back here because not everyone will have everything that I've got listed here. This way you can learn the tricks for only what you have in your house. Each item will include how to clean it for the BIG JOB and then any particular Maintenance it requires.

BASKETS, RATTAN, WICKER, STRAW

BJ: Most baskets; wicker, rattan and straw can be washed*. Remember, we're not soaking then, we're just getting them clean. This is best done outside or if you don't have outside space it can be done in the bathtub or shower. Spray item liberally with vinegar inside, outside, and all around including handle; then rinse.** Shake off excess water and set aside to dry. You may have to rotate the item for it to dry all around.

---

* If the basket has any type of decoration you might try to remove it. If you can't it's, your guess whether it can be cleaned. If the basket is full of silk or artificial flowers remove these and wash separately from basket. Reassemble when dry.

** If the baskets have been in or near the kitchen for any length of time you may want to use the KK to get the grease off them first. If they are really, really greasy, you may have to KK them more than once to get them really, really clean.

CEILING FANS:

BJ: When cleaning anything, you always want to get as close to your work as you can; especially in this case where the fan is above your head. Move any furniture that is under the fan out of the way. Move it far enough away so you can place your ladder properly and not have to stretch or reach very far to get to the blades and housing. If you have carpet under the fan you want to cover it with the shower curtain, same if there is a bed under it.

Put your ladder as shown in the photos if you are right handed (Photo 10.1). Placement of ladder and where you are in relationship to the fan blades is important because it gives you the ability to support the blades with your non-cleaning hand as you clean so you don't break the blade off. If you are right handed, the top of the ladder should be just to the left of the fan's center. Make sure you support the blade at the outside edge with your left hand while you clean with the right. If you are left-handed, just reverse the instructions.

If you break off a blade, replacement brackets are very difficult to find and the bracket cannot be repaired because of the type of metal they are made from. So you may end up with a new fan. (Hmmmmmm.)

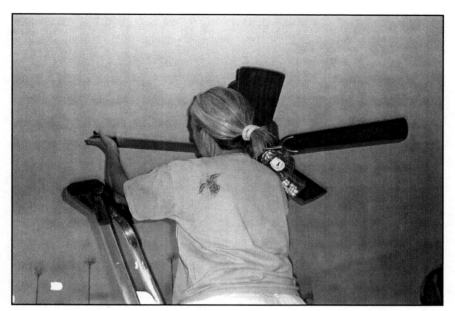

Photo 10.1
***Right Handed Fan Cleaning. Ladder is just to the
left of the center of the fan. If you are left handed the
ladder would be just to the right of the center.***

If your fan blades and housing are exceptionally dirty you may want to dust the big pieces off first with a dry WTR otherwise you are going to make mud when you spray them. Use the KK and start at the top which is that large round thing above the blades; this is the fan housing - spray and wipe until clean with WTR. For the blades, spray top, bottom, and edge of blades very liberally with KK. Use your detail brush to get into the detail of the blade bracket if you have any. Wipe clean. Spray and wipe again if it is not clean. Make sure to get ALL the dirt off the leading edge of the fan, that's the dirtiest edge of the blade. If you have used lots of KK to get the dirt off you may "finish" with vinegar. To find the leading edge of a fan turn the fan on to see which way is it going?

Maintenance: With very few exceptions you can't reach your fan without a ladder so this is where the Swiffer Duster that extends is used. Monthly, or more frequently if the fan runs all the time, bend the duster and dust the top of the blade, also make sure you get the leading edge clean too.

Note: I have run into a few ceiling fans (newer and appearing very expensive) where I couldn't figure out how to get the glass off to clean it. If you have the installation/instruction booklets you get with these, you'll be ahead of the game. Most fans are pretty obvious to get the glass off them.

DISHWASHER

Photo 10.2 is a photo of the dishwasher door fully open. I've included this because very few people seem to clean this poor thing. Hey, it works it heart out to make you life easier, so why not give it a treat and clean it.

With the door open (as in the photo) spray the outside rim (the dirty part) with KK and using your small detail brush get all the food and drips off it. Down close to the hinge may take a few sprays and scrub tries to get it clean. Look for the dirt, you'll see it if you haven't ever cleaned this part before. Keeping this clean should also be part of your maintenance. Get the dirt while it's new – *it's easy.* Wait until it gets old and dried and you got *work* to do.

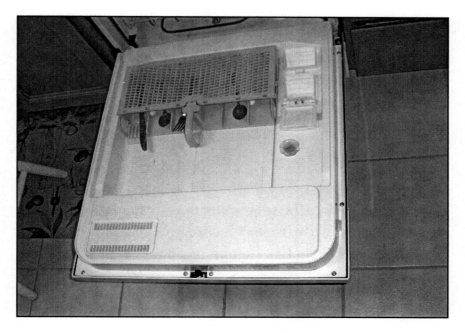

Photo 10.2
Dishwasher Door open. In this photo
you are looking down on the door.

"FINISH" WITH VINEGAR

Not being a chemist I cannot explain the breath and depth of the attributes of vinegar, but you need to make it your best friend, trust me. Any time you have to work to get something clean (KK) you should always finish it with a spray of vinegar and a MFR. Always use white vinegar and never dilute it. Use it full strength. It's so cheap and available, there's no excuse for not putting the "final touch" on a job.

FLOORS – What's on your floor beside dirt?

You may have an assortment of floor types and materials in your house. So you may have to use one or more or all of these methods to get them clean and keep them clean.

Wall-to-Wall Carpet

Typically, when vacuuming carpet with an upright, the machine doesn't get into the **edge** where the carpet meets the wall as well as it should. If you haven't moved your furniture away from the wall recently (as in BJ), your upright hasn't even gotten close to the edge.

BJ: Put your crevice tool on the hose and vacuum the baseboard first, then vacuum where the carpet meets the baseboard. This is called *"edging"* the room. Spray baseboard liberally with KK, use detail brush if the top edge doesn't come clean with just wiping, and don't forget the corners. Vacuum all the carpet where furniture will go using either your upright or the carpet attachment on your canister if you have one. Do your best to return all furniture back into the carpet holes it came out of so you don't make more holes than you want.

Maintenance: Again, what's your threshold for dirt? If you are able to get under most of your furniture with you vacuum (upright or canister) do it. Otherwise, vacuum what you can get to easily, but remember there is dirt under everything, that's why I recommend the BJ at least once a year.

Hard Floors - Tile, laminate, hardwood, linoleum, concrete.

BJ: Vacuum the baseboard, vacuum where the floor meets the baseboard (edging), then the floor. Spray baseboard liberally with KK, use detail brush if the top edge doesn't come clean with just wiping, and don't forget the corners, wash exposed floor. Using the swiffer mop, WTR and KK5:1 do your floors; remember you have to clean the floor until the rag comes up clean. "Finish" with vinegar and a WTR if you had to use KK.

Maintenance: From my experience if most of your floors are hard, I'd invest in a canister with the combination floor attachment. (Photo 1.7) Here's what happens: Because you do not have any carpeting to catch the dust bunnies and hold on to them, every time you walk though a room or a space, you create a whirlwind behind you that swirls the bunnies around. If they happen to migrate under a piece of furniture; later when someone walks past that piece of furniture they create their own whirlwind which could suck the bunny back out. Do you ever wonder where all the dirt has come from right after you just vacuumed? That's what's happening. If you vacuum with the canister and floor piece, you can get under almost everything. If you have to remove the floor piece and thrash the poles under the furniture and suck up those bunnies, you'll find fewer bunnies showing up right after you vacuum if you do this.

Hard Floor with Area Rug Combination

BJ: Area rugs don't usually reach the edge of the room - that why they're called area and not wall to wall. If the rug does not have a lot of furniture on it then fold it or roll it up and move it out of the way. Clean the floor then return rug and vacuum it. If there is furniture all over the rug, move the furniture away from the edge and flip the edge back so you can vacuum and mop the area up to the wall. Dirt migrates under carpets and this area needs to be cleaned on occasion. Return furniture to place.

Maintenance: get your vacuum (either one) *under* the edge of the rug because dirt has migrated there since the last time you cleaned. Small throw rugs should be taken outside and shaken vigorously and laundered with some regularity.

GLASS: All glass, regardless of where it is or what its doing, is cleaned the same way. This includes anything that is crystal.

BJ and Maintenance: Always spray the surface liberally with vinegar and clean it using *2 clean MFR.* One cleans the glass; the second dries and polishes it. Never clean glass with a rag used on anything else, always 2 *clean* MFR. Even if you have to clean something more than once to get it clean and streak free, each time get new MFRs. Once you've paid for the rags you can use them with abandon.

Of Note: If you have been using some of the more popular "window cleaners"; up to now getting large expanses of glass (mirrors, windows, glass doors) clean will take some effort. We have found that when using vinegar after using these other products you may have to wash the glass 3-4-5 or 6 times to get a streak free clean. After you start using vinegar on your glass you will notice that it doesn't get streaky or cloudy like it did before. I have my own theory as to why, but that's not important right now. Just be prepared to clean and re-clean until it is perfect.

When cleaning mirrors hanging over wood furniture, like the dresser mirror, it wouldn't hurt to lay a few rags on the top of the furniture under the mirror. So when you are *liberally* spraying the mirror you're not soaking the top of the piece.

Word of caution: Do not let KK dry on glass or mirror. It will leave a mark.

KNICK-KNACKS:

There are probably more knick-knacks than there are human beings in the world. When cleaning this stuff, give some thought to what it is made of rather than the intrinsic value or what you paid for it.

BJ: If it is a ceramic of any type; glazed or unglazed, think about it, your dishes are ceramics too. You wash them every day, in the dish washer no less, so why not these things. The same thing goes for metal, glass; even lacquer items can be washed. You're not soaking them or scrubbing them with an abrasive; for the most part, you are just spraying them with vinegar or KK (depending on just how dirty they are and what room they came out of) and rinsing them under running water. You're not even drying them. Set them aside and let them dry while cleaning the rest of the room.

For crystal, glass, mirrors, and china, spray with 100% vinegar and rinse in hot water. The hotter the water, the faster it dries with fewer spots. Anything that is intricate (lots of hard to reach nooks and crannies, or delicate) is ideal for being cleaned this way because you're not touching any of the delicate parts.

Down here where I live there is an abundance of things made of wood, with feathers, fur, painted, carved and for the most part dirty. Ideally, this type of ornamentation should be under glass or in a cabinet because they are so difficult to clean.

Wooden objects that are very dusty/dirty can be sprayed with vinegar and blotted dry with a MFR. If there are feathers, lightly spray a MFR with vinegar and gently wipe the feather from the base out to the tip. Try to support the feather so as not to break or bend it. Also don't forget there are two sides to the feather.

Maintenance: Since, we'll assume, everything was washed during the BJ, just dusting most of these things with an MFR sprayed with vinegar will keep them clean – until dusting doesn't work anymore.

LIGHT FIXTURES

BJ: Just how many different types of light fixtures do you think there are? I give up how many are there? There are wall mounted, ceiling mounted, old, new, odd, clean, dirty and then even dirtier.

Remember again to get as close to your work as possible and Oh! let the bulbs cool off before you try to remove them. All light bulbs in every fixture should be removed and washed when doing a BJ.

Whatever you have for light fixtures and you probably have several types in your house, you want to take as much of it apart as you can.

Chandeliers: Pop quiz – How many types of chandeliers do you think there are? I don't have that answer either – I don't even have a clue!

These poor things don't seem to get cleaned very often because they are so intricate, but a newly cleaned chandelier is truly another thing of beauty (right behind a bathroom that you just did a BJ on!)

First make sure you move all furniture away from under fixture so you can get close to the fixture and you eliminate the chance of damaging the furniture. Don't forget to lay the shower curtain on the floor under the fixture. Take the bulbs out, wash them and set them aside to dry.

Prism/Crystal Chandeliers: If you have a chandelier with lots of dangly prisms and strings of crystals; rather than remove them clean them in place. Move any furniture under the fixture out of the way and put your shower curtain on the floor. Get up on your ladder and spray the whole fixture with vinegar, spray it until it is dripping. Using two MFR, on in each hand, begin at the top of the fixture and wipe/dry a slice of it top down. You should get 2 clean rags for each slice or get a clean rag when one gets wet or dirty.

Slabs of Glass: (Photo 10.3) If your chandelier has slabs of glass hanging off the frame, simply remove each piece of glass and stand it on it's long side on the top rack of your dishwasher. Run the light wash cycle with a smidge of soap and let the machine dry them. Clean the rest of the fixture including the chain and re-hang the glass when the room is cleaned.

Photo 10.3
Slabs of Glass Chandelier

Globes: Remove the globe, then the bulb, wash in very hot water and set aside. Spray the rest of the fixture and wipe clean with MFR, use detail brush if necessary. Don't forget to wipe the chain if there is one.

Upturned/Hanging bowls or shades: (Photo 10.4) these types of fixtures usually have a plastic, ceramic or metal ring that is holding the bowl or shade in place. In Photos 10.5 and 10.6 when you look into the shade if there are threads on the outside of the ceramic thing that you screw the bulb into – then you have a ring. First remove

Photo 10.4
Upturned/Downturned Bowls.
These will have rings holding the shade in place.

Photo 10.5
Threads on Light Socket.
If you have these you have to remove the ring in order
to remove the shade. Righty – tighty; lefty – loosey.

Photo 10.6
Ring Holding Shade. This ring is
either plastic, ceramic or metal.

the bulb, then the ring, this particular ring is white plastic (remember righty – tighty; lefty – loosey). When clean and dry, replace the shade and put the ring back on; but do not crank the ring too tight, you don't want to break the ring or the shade.

Maintenance: I wouldn't do much with most of these types of fixtures except make sure you vacuum it out occasionally. You'll be surprised how many dead bugs end up in here.

Any light bulb/fixture in the bathroom is going to get dirty quickly. Depending on what you use here (powder, hairspray, perfume) you may have to wash these every time you do any maintenance. Remember, whatever goes up must come down and it's going to come down right on top of your hot lights and be cooked.

Ceiling Mounted Fixtures: There are way too many types of ceiling mounted fixtures to list or even describe in any detail. For that reason I've included 3 for a quickie overview.

Photo 10.7 is the type with a sheet of plastic that hangs on a lip flush with the ceiling. These are tricky to get down and even trickier to get up if they are of any age. These pieces of plastic get brittle in a few years so when you try to remove them, they break.

To remove one of these get up on a ladder, gently push up one end of the plastic and try to fold it ever so slightly like a taco, (it is now narrower than the hole) elevate one end and drop the other end down through the hole. Ok, if you got it out congrats! If it broke while trying this maneuver, save the pieces and take them to the hardware store and have them cut a new one using the old one as a

Photo 10.7
Flush Mount Ceiling Light Fixture.
Usually found in kitchens and bathrooms.

template. You want to use the old one as a template because no matter how many times I've measured for one of the these; I've never gotten it right on the first try. When you buy a new one there are probably several types available – get the one that is most flexible - this will be the easiest to get back in.

If you got it out in one piece; wash it, let it dry, and put it back up. Now you have the same challenge in reverse. Get up close to the hole and flex the sheet slightly, like a taco, and slide one end up into the space, then the other end, then let it go. Good luck!!! If you have any burned out tubes or bulbs up there, now is the time to replace them.

Photo 10.8
Ceiling Mount Boxed Fixture

Photo 10.8 is pretty straight forward right after you figure out how this fixture is attached. The photo shows one end with a screw. This screw is about 4 inches long and on the other end are two flat metal pieces facing the inside of the box. Get up there close, remove the screw, but keep a hand on the box. When the screw is out (put it in your pocket, do not drop it) Get a good grip on the box and push the box away from you, still holding it flush to the ceiling, far enough for the other end of the box to release the box from the fixture. Voila!! If you have any serious doubts, that you can't do this alone then enlist a friend or one of your taller kids, a husband, neighbor – anyone to hold the other end.

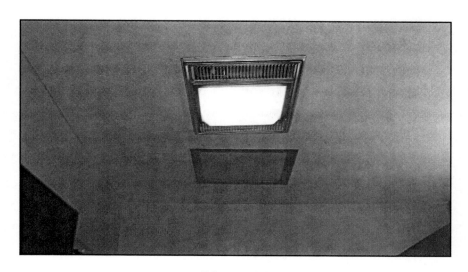

Photo 10.9
Light/Exhaust Fan Combo. Usually found
in bathrooms and laundry rooms.

Photo 10.10
Light/Exhaust Fan Combo Open.

Photo 10.9 and 10.10 These two photos is a bathroom light fixture/exhaust fan combination. In the BJ bathroom section this is one of the exhaust fans that you brush, with the fan on, to get rid of the fuzzies, but it has a light. If you pull on the rim, around the glass, down (from the sides without the exhaust grill) you'll expose the light. If you squeeze the metal pieces the rim and glass is hanging from you can remove the whole thing. If you remove the light bulb there is a screw in the middle that is holding the rest of the assembly to the ceiling. If you remove this screw you can actually remove the entire metal frame and clean the whole assemble and possibly up into the ceiling (where all those fuzzies have gone). Reassemble in reverse.

MICROWAVE OVENS: This explanation will be primarily for the microwave oven (MWO) mounted over the range. However, if you have a MWO on the counter this section shows how to clean the inside and outside of the unit.

There are four separate pieces to MWO that you are concerned with: the exhaust grill on top, the inside, the front panel including the door, and the underside of the unit.

The Exhaust Grill: BJ: Most MWO have a built in exhaust system that blows out the top of the unit, usually toward you. The vent can be a plastic grill that is removable so it can be cleaned. If you didn't know it was removable and you haven't cleaned it in a while you've got some work to do. The grill is held on either side with screws on the top or two screws on the front.

Photo 10.11 is the unit that usually has 4 screws on the top of the unit holding it in place. Remove all four screws and immediately

Photo 10.11
MWO Screws on Top of Unit. 2 to 4 screws

put them in the cabinet over the MWO so you know where they are when you're trying to put it back on. First, open the MWO door, remove the screws, and then remove the grill. Some models require that the grill be slid slightly to the side in order to get it off. If you still have the instruction book that came with the unit, I'd refer to it for reference.

Photo 10.12 shows the unit that has two tiny screws on the face of the grill. These can be tricky to remove because you have to remember to PUSH the screwdriver INTO the screw to get it out. If you do not press hard enough into the screw, you will strip the head and never get it out. Remember, PUSH while TURNING. PUUUSSSH!

Photo 10.12
MWO Screws on Front of Unit. 2 very long screws

Again, put the screws in the cabinet above the MWO so you don't lose them.

If this is the first time you've removed the grill since it was installed, you may have to spray, soak, and scrub this thing more than once to get it clean.

There are several more types of MWO vents out there and most of them require you to remove screws to get at the filter and dirt that is behind it.

Another type of MWO has a solid piece that drops down forward, the venting is going straight up toward the ceiling. Some of these have screen filters inside. Remove these and clean them periodically. Put it in the dishwasher, bottom shelf, to get it clean without any work if they fit.

Maintenance: I would suggest that you remove this grill and clean it when doing the BJ but if you do lots of cooking you need to clean it more frequently. If you are tall enough you can see the grease accumulating on the grill. If you are not that tall step up on a chair occasionally and check it out. Remember: Grease can harden into cement and if you have enough of it, it will start smelling, like old grease.

Inside the MWO: BJ and Maintenance: If your unit has a plate that revolves, leave it in the unit for now. Spray the inside with KK, get a soaking dripping wet clean WTR and put in oven, close door and run for 2 minutes. The water in the rag will boil, creating steam which will soften everything that is baked on in there. Don't remove rag immediately, let it sit while you clean the outside and underside. When you get back to this, after you cleaned the next two parts, remember that rag is still HOT!!! Use the plate to dump the rag into the sink and now wipe out the oven. If you don't have a revolving plate in your MWO use anything *but* your fingers to remove the rag, it is HOT, HOT HOT! (you just boiled it!) If everything doesn't come out the first time do it again. I've had ovens that had to be steamed several times to get the crud out.

The front panel including door: BJ and Maintenance: Spray the whole front (or outside) of the unit with KK and using your detail brush to get *all the gunk* out of the corners and grooves. Do not forget the backside of the handle. Do not use anything abrasive on door, it is plastic inside and out and scratches easily. Wipe clean and respray/clean if you left anything behind.

Underside: BJ and Maintenance: (Photo 10.13) the underside of MWO is about the dirtiest place in a kitchen. Just about everything ever cooked on the range has splashed up on the underside. Look up under there. There should be a light (is it working?) and screens (1, 2 or 3) and lots of grease. Use a screwdriver and remove the cover over the light, clean and put aside. Remove the screens and leave to soak in the sink or put in dishwasher, bottom shelf, and clean that way. Using plenty of KK spray and using the green scrubby, scrub until clean as it was the day it was installed. Open the door to clean the bottom of the door. It's usually crusted with stuff.

BJ: NOTE: Don't forget that before you got to the MWO you cleaned the cabinet above it and when you've finished you still have the wall under it and the stove. Do not "Finish" anything until the whole slice is clean, ceiling to floor.

Photo 10.13
Underside of MWO

PICTURES: Framed with glass, oils, needlework, plaques. What else do you have hanging on your walls?

BJ: Framed with Glass: Pictures with glass should be removed from the wall and laid on a flat surface to clean. If the picture/mirror is too big or too heavy it will have to be cleaned in place. Never spray a picture while it is hanging up. If the vinegar runs down between the glass and the frame, the mat or picture will soak it up (wicking) and may ruin whatever it is. Lay it on a flat surface, floor, table, whatever, spray the glass and all four sides of the frame. Using 2 MFR, one to wash, the second to dry, clean glass and frame. Don't forget the corners.

Is the frame carved? Are there ridges or detail? If yes, then you need your detail brush to get all the dust out. If the frame is intricately carved, spray the frame heavily with vinegar, brush all the detail then wad up a clean MFR and press it into the carving to dry it. Now clean the glass.

Hold picture up and move it around to make sure you did a good job and it is not smeared or streaky. If you have been using some "glass" cleaners, which I will not mention by name, you may have to clean the glass (and mirrors) several times to get a smear free, streak free clean. When the front is clean don't forget to turn it over and use the wetter of your MFR and wipe the back. Do any edges back there and the wire. Check the wall where it was hanging and make sure there are no cooties there, if so wipe, rehang picture. You do this to every picture in the house. Wait until you have finished the job to go back and make sure all pictures and mirrors are straight.

Maintenance: Wiping with a MFR sprayed with vinegar will keep it clean, if you can't easily reach it use the Swiffer Duster. Of course, we're assuming it's been cleaned in a BJ.

Oils: There are several opinions on how to clean an oil painting. If you think about what you have, oils are very durable, even paintings done with acrylics. Unfortunately most people have never done anything but lightly dust their oils and they now have a house load of dull, dirty oils.

Let me tell you what I have done for, oh, only about 40 years. I have several oils painted by family members and they are very dear to me so I'd never do anything that would damage them in any way. However, they do get cleaned on a regular basis. I lightly spray a clean MFR with vinegar and I wipe the canvas, yeah! That's what

I do. There is no damage to the picture and the colors are as bright as they were when they were painted over 40 years ago. Caution is to be used if the painting has thick globs of paint and the surface is very irregular and craggy. You have to be very careful not to snag your rag on any of them and possibly tear it off.

If you are an art restorer, you probably just threw yourself out the closest window after reading the above suggestions. We'll miss you. Dear Reader, if you do happen to have an Old Masters' original painting worth millions, do not use my suggestions. For the other 800,000,000 other readers just clean them!!

If the frame is carved or very intricate, this should be cleaned before you do the canvas. Don't forget the back and the wire.

Maintenance: MFR with vinegar or Swiffer

BJ: Fabric Art: Anything that is needlework, knitted, woven, crocheted. If it is framed and on a wall you'd be wise to have glass on it because you can never 'clean' it. Clean the frame, all sides and back taking care not to touch the piece and move on.

Woven, knitted, crocheted things I'd try to get into the dryer and knock the dust off that way. If all else fails vacuum piece with the upholstery attachment and then wipe with a MFR with vinegar.

Helpful Hint: Some houses we clean we refer to as "booby traps" because of the way the pictures are hung. I have seen pictures hung with everything imaginable except chewing gum, but then again, I haven't been in every house yet!

Don't make your life or the job of keeping your house clean any more difficult than it already is. Some day, say to yourself; 'Self,

I'm going to make all my pictures regulation". Regulation is: eyelet screws, picture wire and a *real* picture hanger. Wow, novel idea! You can go to the hardware store and buy picture hanging kits that have everything for various sized pictures and fix them all in one fell swoop.

How to re-hang a picture: How many times have you thought you 'got' the picture on the hook, let go of the picture and crash, it hits the floor? I've done it myself, a few hundred times, until I figured out a fool proof way to do it right. If, and only if, your frame and the hanging assembly is regulation (two eyelet screws and wire) hold the picture in one hand and hold the wire in the other, now if you can see what you're doing, good; or feel your way to get the wire *on* the 'regulation' hook before you let go of the picture. If you have a very large picture or mirror use two people. One holds the frame in front of them with both hands, one on either side, and the other person 'hangs' the wire on the hook or hooks before the holder lets go. *Don't go fishing.* That's what we call trying to get the wire on the hook and *hope* it's there before you let go of it.

PUMICE STONE: Like the scrubby, the pumice stone can destroy a porcelain fixture; but, if used properly, it is the only way to get mineral deposits out of toilets and from around the sink drains. I prefer the soft stones and small pieces. If you have a hard water problem, you will need to use the stone every time you clean the toilet. Like the rest of the maintenance suggestions, if you keep on top of the dirt you have an easier job keeping your house clean.

Before you use the stone make sure the fixture (toilet, sink, tub) is clean.

In the toilet, it's the ring that appears at the water level. Using two hands feel what needs the work and feel when it is clean.

Around sink drains you may find a dark ring that doesn't move when you use the scrubbie. This is mineral deposit, use the stone here. Move cautiously and only work on the stain.

Once you scratch a fixture you have no remedy; you live with it or buy a new sink (toilet, tub).

RANGES (Gas, electric, glass top, whatever) The night before you do the BJ you should run the self-clean cycle of your oven so you can finish the inside as part of the job. If your oven isn't self-cleaning, I'd save this job for another day. If you clean the oven before you do the BJ then the *whole* job is done when the BJ is done.

For starters, remove everything that you can from the range (knobs, burner parts) and put in the sink filled with hot, hot, hot water and a big shot of KK. The knobs come off. If they haven't been off in a while you're going to have to work them off.

Electric Range: If the elements are removable, do this, and put them aside. Put all the burner rings and drip pans in the sink with the knobs. If the pans and rings are old and beyond cleaning, replace them. After you reassemble the range make sure the knobs are in the right positions and then turn the burners on high. If they are dirty, they will start smoking, burning off the grease; when they stop smoking, turn them off. This is also a good thing to do – if they work, the elements are in properly.

THE LOST ART OF HOUSE CLEANING

Gas: The metal that the pots sit on can be cleaned. Put them in the sink. If they are bigger than your sink you may have to rotate them. However, they can be sent through the dishwasher.

The bottom drawer is usually a broiler in gas units. Take out whatever you can and clean it.

Glass Top: These are not easy to keep clean especially if you boil something over at the beginning of cooking. You can 't clean them until the glass has cooled which is pretty late.

For serious stuff on the glass, use some of the cleaners made specifically for these ranges. We also use a straight edged razor to scrape the stuff up. Be careful that you do not gouge the glass. After you get the glass clean, 'finish' it with vinegar.

The Bottom Drawer: Most ranges have a bottom drawer that is used to store pots, pans and a lot of crumbs. Pull it completely out. If you haven't pulled this out before, you need to pull it as far out as it goes then lift up.

If you have one of those newer ranges where the bottom drawer is another oven – do not touch.

BJ: The range needs to be pulled out from the wall so you can clean all the stuff that has dribbled down the sides. Do not pull it out until you have finished everything in that slice down to the drawer.

Pull the range out as far as you can which will be determined by how long the lines (gas or electric) are on the back. The easiest grip is to open the oven door slightly and drag it toward you. Most ranges are not that heavy and are easily moved, however, if you have one of those restaurant type ranges you will need 3 men and a gorilla to move it.

Photo 10.14
Sides of Range Pulled Out

Photo 10.15
Floor (and dirt) Exposed Under Range

Photo 10.16
Walls Next to Range. As dirty as sides of range.

If you notice lots of food stuff has dribbled down the sides of the range (Photo 10.14), there is probably dribble on the sides of the cabinet it was wedged between. These need to be cleaned as well. If you found more than you were expecting on the floor under the range after you pulled it out, I'd suggest you vacuum up the big chunks before you spray anything. (Photo 10.15 and 10.16)

Remembering The PATH; when cleaning the range (or anything for that matter) you work top down. If you ran the self-clean cycle you'll want to finish the inside. Spray anything that did not come clean with KK and let it soak. Use the green scrubbie and scrub until it all comes off. It will, it will just take time. After it's clean, finish with vinegar. Turn the oven on when you're finished and let it heat up to burn off the vinegar. This should only take about 15 minutes.

When it's all clean in and out, push it back against the wall. Finish the range with vinegar and put all the parts back where they came from. Make sure you put the knobs on the correct stems.

Maintenance: If doesn't matter what you have for a range, gas, electric, glass top, it should be cleaned after every use. If you make another meal on a dirty range the heat just bakes the dirt on to an immovable mass, now it's never coming off. Remember the 3 spray bottles under the sink, which is close to the range? Only use KK on the range and let it soak.

After the dishes are finished, do your range. If you have really trashed the drip pans under the burners put them in the dishwasher with the rest of the stuff you dirtied. If you fried dinner, the back of the range where the clock and knobs are is dirty too.

REFRIGERATOR: There are a few things about refrigerators that are most often overlooked when cleaning them.

The Gasket: Take this book with you and go open your refrigerator and look at that white gasket (rubber piece) that goes all the way around the door on the inside. Peek into it, peek into the piece running across the top. Now if you are of regular height (under 6 feet tall) you will probably need to stand on a chair or step ladder to see this. This should be clean – in order to do that, you have to clean it. Remember, the falling dirt, it doesn't know a refrigerator from the cabinet top. If you found slime on top of your cabinets you're going to find slime in this gasket. Ok, but more interesting than that is get off your chair and get down on your knees and peek at the under side of the door. Every time something spilled on the floor near the refrigerator chances are pretty good that some of it splashed up – right under the door and it's been there since Ralphy was 3 and the bottle of grape juice slipped out of his hands. Who said kids don't leave us memories? (By the way, Ralphy is graduating from college in the spring.) Fill the gasket with KK and let it sit for a few minutes, using your detail brush get all that slime out of there, do not use anything sharp on this thing, if you puncture it you're not going to feel good about getting it clean. You may need to spray and brush several times – clean it until it's clean. Use WTRs for this job.

Note: I don't want you to think I'm compulsive or anal about dirt but you have to agree that some things need to be *cleaned at least once in their lifetime.*

BOTTOM VENT: Some times when we go in to clean a house we make bets on how big the 'cat' is that's under the refrigerator. The 'cat' is the fur and dust we take off the vanes; there is enough dirt, dust and animal fur to mold a decent sized cat – but the bet is how big is that cat going to be? If you have any animals; cat, dog, gerbil, bunny, (teenagers excluded here) you're going to have a lot of hair under there on the vanes. With enough hair or dust on the vanes your motor is gasping for air trying to do its job. Really! Put your ear on the side and listen to it wheezing and gasping.

Photo 10.17 is the vent on the bottom of a refrigerator that has the freezer on the bottom and it is a drawer. The piece that is outlined comes off. These are not the easiest to remove, but they do come off. After you get it off, it needs to go outside and get washed. It really

Photo 10.17
Refrigerator (with Bottom Freezer Drawer) Vent Cover

probably needs several rounds of KK, brush, rinse, KK, brush, rinse. Now you have to lie down on the floor and get your vacuum with crevice tool and suck all that stuff out of there.

If you haven't done this job ever, since you got the refrigerator, you may notice also on the back of the refrigerator that dust is coming out that back vent – that needs to be cleaned too. If you can get that grill panel off the back, you might try to clean what you can.

After you finished cleaning the unit, put your ear on the side again and listen to the sigh of relief. Think of a dirty refrigerator bottom like trying to breath with cotton balls stuffed up your nose. Hey, the refrigerator doesn't have an opposing thumb so it's relying on you to keep it healthy.

HANDLE: Handles, sometimes, can be a challenge; especially if the front of the handle is white, or supposed to be white, and the back side is black or very dark grey. This is a job for KK and the scrubbie. Spray lots of KK on the scrubbie and start cleaning, up and down, up and down, wipe, spray scrubbie again and continue. I have *not* had a handle that did not come clean. If you have an older refrigerator that has a metal edge on the handle, you could have thanksgiving dinner in there from your first year in the house. This is where I use the dental tools, if you do not have them you can use the tip of a steak knife or paring knife; anything sharp and pointy, anything that will get the slime out.

SCRUBBIE: Like I wrote in Chapter 2, these will either be your salvation or the bane of your life. Before using the scrubbie on anything, do a small test to see if it will scratch. If it does, don't use it.

When doing porcelain fixtures, tubs, sinks, toilets, you can pretty much use it with abandon. For fiberglass, imitation marble, Corian; you want to use it flat handed. Lay the scrubbie in the palm of your hand and apply even pressure cleaning the walls.

If you have brass hardware on you sinks and tubs, do not use the scrubbie. This will scratch the finish. Chrome hardware is tough and will just shine when it's clean. Use it on glass shower doors; use caution if the doors are plastic or acrylic.

We use the scrubbie, for that matter, several when doing a BJ in a kitchen. We also use it on cabinets. Sometimes there is so much gunk on the edges of the doors, where the hand touches the door to open it and on the top edge where all the grease landed on it, we use the scrubbie. You may have to spray and scrub until you get through the dirt. You know you're through the dirt when you touch it and it is not sticky. If it's still sticky, it's not clean, do it again.

If you happen to remove the finish and/or color on the door, repair it with Old English Dark Furniture Oil.

SILKS (FLOWERS, TREES, PLANTS)

When I become president, this is the second thing I'm going to outlaw (the first is louvered doors in or near the kitchen). In principle, they may add value to a décor, but since so few people know how to properly clean them they're disgustingly dirty for the most part. All silk and plastic flower arrangements, plants, trees, vines, branches, sticks, etc., should be taken outside and thoroughly washed. If these things were in the kitchen, then you will probably have to clean them with KK to get the grease and dust off. If they were anywhere else in your house, you can get them clean with just vinegar. I have an issue with some of the 'artificial plant cleaners'. You keep spraying it on them but how does the dirt come off?

BJ: Hopefully, you are able to take all these things outside to clean. Otherwise you'll be cleaning them in the tub or shower. Spray liberally with vinegar making sure to get down into the arrangement. If you are cleaning a tree that is higher than you are tall you have to lower the top so that you can spray the vinegar on the tree in the same direction that the dirt fell on it; from the top. If you tip the tree over against a chair or table you should be eye-to-top with the tree. When you rinse it with the hose do it from this same angle. Make sure you empty any water that may have gotten into the base. If the tree is in a straw, wicker, rattan basket, vinegar this too and rinse.

AAAGGGGHHH!!! Sphagnum moss stuffed at the base of trees and plants. I have nightmares about this stuff. When this stuff is new, like, less than 6 months old, it is attractive. When it is 3, 5, 9, 15 years old, it is disgusting. Have you ever cleaned it???? No, you haven't. Because you can't!!! Throw it out, out, out and don't replace it unless you are going to replace it every 6 months. Throw it out if you can. If that stuff is old enough when you pick it up it will disintegrate and shed all the way to the basket. Uck! Nasty stuff when old.

Maintenance: Not much to do with these things except wash them or chuck it.

SWIFFER MOP – The bigger mop (which is dark blue) is absolutely necessary if you have a lot of hard floor. I have about a dozen of them and we can cover 1500 to 2000 square feet in under an hour.

The only limitation is that the pole tends to break with extensive use. We use ours 5 days a week, so we've mopped a boat load of floor and I'm not surprised that it breaks. The FIX for this is; go to your local hardware store and get a length of ¾ white PVC plastic pipe. Drop the pipe over what's left of the pole and tape on with Duct Tape (long live DT). It will last for another couple of years.

We put a WTR on the mop and do the floor, when the WTR gets dirty or too wet just pull it off and put on a clean one. We also use these to mop walls with a MFR.

WINDOW TREATMENTS (curtains/drapes, shutters, shades, venetian/vertical blinds,)

CURTAINS/DRAPES (valances, swags, anything fabric on or around a window)

My suggestions is *do not* put anything that is fabric in or near the kitchen unless you can take it down *and wash it* on a regular basis. Again, I ask, how dirty does something have to get before you think it needs to be cleaned? Hey, they look good, but that's only because they are so high up you can't see *just how dirty they are*. But, I've been up there and they are dirty! Think about it; if the cabinet tops get greasy and slimy, why wouldn't the curtains? You think that droplet of grease is going to fall around the valance? Think not! If you ever take them down dispose of them as hazardous waste. If you were to set them on fire it would take a week for the fire to go out. They're going up like a pan of bacon grease. Remember dirt doesn't discriminate.

If your curtains, drapes or valances were professionally installed there isn't much you can do to clean them unless you want to send them out to be dry cleaned. Unfortunately, this can be expensive. You can vacuum them in place and if they are dark colored you can spray a MFR with vinegar and wipe them. You will take a lot of the dust off them and they will look somewhat better from the floor.

If you have fabric valances nailed to a wood frame you can vacuum and wipe as above.

BJ: If your window coverings are washable take them down and have them ready to rehang after you finish the BJ in that room.

Of note: If you have an extensive expanse of drapery in a room, occasionally look behind them and up. We've found lots of cooties, spider webs and other creepy crawlies back there where no one has ever gone since they were put up there.

Maintenance: If you can't wash what's hanging on your windows, there's not much more you can do for maintenance.

SHUTTERS:

Bless the soul that invented the wide blade shutter. He or she will be eternally admired, especially by everyone that has to clean them.

Even better than the wide blade shutter is the wide blade shutter that doesn't have that bar down the middle that moves the blades up and down. The newest generation has no bar. Who said you had to die to get to heaven?

Even though they are the easiest window covering to keep clean you still have to clean them.

BJ: If the shutter blade is excessively dusty you will make the job easier if you vacuum them first with the round brush attachment on your vacuum. Open the shutter out, vacuum the blades from the back side, and while you have the vac in your hands, turn around and vac the window sill which is usually full of cooties or some other dead bugs. Now you spray both sides of the blades with KK and clean them using MFR from the inside (the side without the bar) making sure you wipe both sides of each blade, the frame, and *that* bar on the front.

Maintenance: If you stay on top of them they can be easily swiffered, but peek inside frequently to see what has died inside there and suck them up.

SHADES: There isn't much to say about window shades. They are either good or they need to be replaced.

VENETIAN BLINDS:

What you got???? Wide blade, narrow blade, wood, composite, plastic, metal, colored to match the décor, silver, you painted yourself (agghhh!) new, old? Come on you can tell me, because I've cleaned at least one of each of those and a few hundred of some of them.

BJ: First you've got to take them down so you'll probably need your ladder. Do you have a valance that is a blind slat? Good luck getting them off without breaking the little brackets that hold them on. If you happen to break them (which we have broken quite a few of) try gluing magnets on the back of the slat to hold it on the blind.

If you can clean them outside then that is where they're going. If you don't have an outside space you can do them in the shower. This will take some maneuvering or… you can just throw them out and get something easier to clean, like wide blade shutters. Ok, so if you're not going to throw them out, you're going to have to clean them.

Look at Photo 10.18. That's a venetian blind hung from bungee cords from the porch of the house. You can also hang them over a fence or wall and your last option is to lay them on the shower curtain on the ground and clean them there.

If you can hang them from something and have access to both sides, like in the picture, you just spray the blind with KK, make sure you turn the slats so you get the whole blade wet, watch the dirt start dripping off the blind, then spray with your hose until the water runs clean. It's preferred if the blind hangs at an angle, this way the water runs off and they dry faster.

If you cannot hang them as shown in the photo you will need to spray on side of the blind, rotate the blades in the other direction, and then spray the other side. Whether hanging on a fence or laying on the shower curtain you will have to flip them over *and* change the direction of the slats, don't forget to rinse both sides also. It is preferred if the blind hangs at an angle; this way the water runs offr and they dry faster.

If your only option is cleaning them in the tub you have a lot more work to get the job done. That was the way I cleaned the blinds in my mother's house growing up. I have seen some gadgets

Photo 10.18
Venetian Blind Hanging Outside to dry after it was cleaned.

in gadget magazines with suction cups you can stick to your shower walls to hold the blind, but I've only seen these for mini-blinds. If you do use these, make sure you flip the blind to spray the other side and turn the slats in the other direction. Rinse both sides.

Maintenance: Venetian blinds need to be kept clean on a regular basis, and yes, that means work. We dust them using the Swiffer Duster. Turn the blades down and dust moving the duster from side to side making sure you bang into the strings. This way you get the dust that hides behind the string. Then turn the blades up and with one hand pull the blind away from the window and with the duster fully extended brush down. By doing this second step you cleaned the back edge of the blind slat so that when the slats are open the back edge is clean. This maneuver takes some practice, but when you see the result it's worth trying to master.

VERTICAL BLINDS

There are a lot of verticals here where I live, but I'm not sure what their population is outside of Arizona; but in the event you have them, this is how to clean them - it's really rather simple.

BJ: Draw the blinds fully closed and turn blades to one side, spray with KK5/1 and then turn blades the other way and spray. Starting at one end, using 2 MFR one in either hand start at the top sandwiching the blind between your two hands (plus rags) and in one motion move down to the bottom of the slat. Move across blind in one direction (don't skip any). (Photo 10.19) You should be prepared to clean the window behind the blind when you get done with this job because more than likely some of the KK5/1 got through to the glass.

Photo 10.19
Vertical Blind Cleaning

Maintenance: There isn't too much to do for these except Swiffer them on occasion.

WOOD FURNITURE:

General Information: We clean wood furniture with vinegar and if necessary the detail brush and sometimes even the scrubbie and use MFR almost exclusively to clean, dry and polish.

When we do a BJ on a house the customer is made to understand we do not polish any furniture as part of the job. Invariably though, when the customer sees the job done they comment about the furniture being "polished". "No, we didn't polish your furniture we just cleaned it --- with vinegar!" The effect is dramatic. Whatever the piece is; table, dresser, bureau, china cabinet, table or chair, spray the whole thing with vinegar and wipe with a MFR. If there are corners, edges or ridges, you need to get into them with the detail brush. When doing a coffee or end table you can spray the whole thing then wipe it clean but if you are doing a large piece of furniture, like a china cabinet or dresser, I'd suggest you do it in sections, again top to bottom, moving in one direction. Heavily carved furniture shows the most dramatic effect when cleaned. Once you get those 56 to 127 years of dust out of the design it looks brand new. If the design is deep and very detailed; bunch a clean FMR and press it into the design to suck up the vinegar (and the dirt). Use another clean MFR to finish it off.

A word of caution: I've had the opportunity to clean some very old and well used chairs and tables. The chairs are usually old wood rockers and have been used every day, sometimes all day, for the last 71 years. The arms on these will have about 1/8 inch of body oil and acid deposited on them just simply as a result of use. The test is to scrape the surface of the arm with your thumbnail, if you get a glob of slime on your nail, it's gotta go.

This is also the test for kitchen cabinets. Scratch the edge of the door where everyone touches them to open them with your thumb nail. We call this the "slime test". If it passes the test; you now have a wad of slime on your nail, clean it as directed below.

Clean any slimy wood surface by spraying liberally with KK and use a clean scrubbie, flat handed, and keep spraying and scrubbing and wiping until you get down to clean wood. It's clean when it is no longer sticky or tacky. After you do the arms you will have to do the rest of the chair, but the result will be worth it. You'll probably have to polish it when you're done, but it's about time don't you think? If, as a function of cleaning the slime off the chair arms it appears the color has lightened, sometimes significantly; it probably has. See below for the "fix". You should finish with vinegar. Especially large expanses of wood like kitchen cabinet doors.

The same thing happens to wood dining room tables that have been used for generations. You may find the body slime spots (do the Slime Test) where mom and dad sat every night for the 63 years that they were married. (Please don't take offense, that's life.)

Don't start the job though if you can't finish it. Don't think you can clean just a 'spot' or two and it's going to be OK, because it won't. You start it, you'll have to finish it, the whole table top, at least.

The FIX: If it happens that you take the finish off something wood trying to get it clean don't throw yourself off the bridge. Take heart, faint soul, what you need to get is some Old English "Dark" furniture polish. Very carefully put a dab on a WTR and gently wipe the spot that lost the color. You're trying to get the spot to match the rest of the surface. So you need to do this building up to the match. If you just slap a rag drenched in the dark oil you're not going to be happy with the result. Gently keep wiping the area until the colors match. Magic!! Well almost, but it works. This is also the remedy for those kitchen cabinet doors that lost the finish (and color) trying to get them clean. If the piece is old enough you might give some thought to refinish it. Of course, again, if this is a priceless antique that came over on the Mayflower and has been passed down for the last 10 generations, you might want to watch the Antiques Roadshow – they say don't refinish.

Be careful what you do with the rag with the stain on it. You don't want to get this stuff on anything else (Pssst, look at your fingers). If you think you'll be using the stain again in the future put it in a small zip lock bag and use it again later.

NOTE: As initially pointed out when doing the BIG JOB we don't move any large pieces of furniture like china cabinets, armoires, bureaus or entertainment centers that are loaded. But there is definitely dirt behind all of them, especially if you have not moved them since you moved in.

Next time you clean them out (You do clean them out occasionally?) and before you reload it, just move it far enough away from the wall to let your canister wand fit behind it. Also, keep this in mind when you move. Before you settle your furniture and load it up leave enough space to clean behind it.

Maintenance: Dusting most wood furniture with a MFR sprayed with vinegar is sufficient to keep it clean between BJ's. However, how the piece of furniture is used will dictate how much work it will require to maintain it.

RECLINERS: I was surprised the first time I turned a recliner over to clean under and behind and found *the interior of the chair* just absolutely packed full of cat hair. Apparently the kitty that lived here liked hiding under the chair and over the years, the inside became clogged with its fur. Even if you don't have a cat when you do your BJ, you turn these upside down just as you would a sofa and get all the cooties.

GLASS TOPPED TABLES: There are basically 2 types of 'glass topped' tables: One has just a *slab of glass* for the top, the other has *glass inset* into metal or wood. (**PSST:** make sure you have read GLASS here in the NG)

Slab of Glass:

BJ: Whether a full sized dining room table or coffee/end table the whole piece of glass comes off the base during the BJ.

Dining room table: This job should take 2 men and a gorilla or 4 women. The way we do it is to line up 3-4 armless chairs along one long side of the table, close together just beyond the edge of the table; with two people on each end lift the glass and stand it on it's side on the chairs. One of the four that moved the glass now moves to behind the chairs and holds the glass while someone else washes what is the underside of the glass. This is also when you wash the table base to the floor, move it out of the way, vacuum/mop the floor, put it back where you want it and then get everyone back to replace the top on the base. Make sure everyone has clean MFR in their hands so they don't smear what was just cleaned. After you have the glass where you want it, you can now clean the top side of the table.

Maintenance: If you did a good job cleaning the underside of the glass during the BJ you'll only have to do some touch-up on the underside as it gets dirty.

Wood/metal tables with glass inset in the top:

BJ: For some reason these tables don't get the attention they require, especially if this is your coffee table and everyone that walks into your house sees it. That piece of glass *does* come out and should be cleaned on both sides. That thin ridge that it sits on, that caught every crumb that ever touched it, needs to be cleaned. Cleaned may mean scrubbing several times with KK and your small detail brush to get the gunk off or even scraping the gunk off.

From the underside of the table gently push the piece of glass up and grab the edge and take it out. Clean both sides and clean the ridge it sits on. Holding the glass with MFR (so you don't get it smeared) rest the end of the glass on the edge and get down and put your hand up the opening and catch the glass and let it down gently.

Maintenance: Obviously you will clean the top of the table when doing you maintenance. That ridge needs to be cleaned as it gets dirty. If you're looking for the dirt you'll know when it has to be cleaned again.

Postface

Well, that's about all I have to say, for now. There's really a lot more where this came from, but I think this is about all anyone can handle for the moment.

I know there's a lot of information in this book, even though it's a small book. I'm confident you'll able to get the hang of what I've presented here and hopefully it will help you make for a happier home (and homeowner).

Thanks for reading, enjoy the clean, and if the river doesn't rise and the bridge doesn't wash out you can see me at my website **www.thelostartofhousecleaning.com** where I've uploaded real time cleaning demonstrations from the Nitty Gritty. The first demonstration is the "Range Slice in the Kitchen". Additional demonstrations will be uploaded as they are produced.

Love,
Jan
the "Head Rag Dragger"

Shopping List

Tear this page out and take it with you to shop for the supplies you'll need to do the job.

CLEANING PRODUCTS

> ➢ **Krud Kutter** – 1 Gallon. (Ace, Home Depot, Lowes)
>
> ➢ **White Vinegar** - 1 Gallon (any store)
>
> ➢ **Soft Scrub with Bleach** – Any store

TOOLS

> ➢ **Spray bottles** (9) I buy the cheapies anywhere ($.98)
>
> ➢ **White terry cloth rags** (5 doz.). Sam's Club in packages of 60
>
> ➢ **Microfiber rags** (4 doz.). Sam's in packages of 24
>
> ➢ **Small detail brush** – Hardware dept. of stores
>
> ➢ **Medium detail brush** – Anywhere
>
> ➢ **Scotch Brite Scouring Pads** (NO sponge) Prefer Sams
>
> ➢ **Pumice Stone** – Cleaning supplies, without the handle
>
> ➢ **Grit cloth** – Paint department near the sandpaper
>
> ➢ **Vacuum** – Ideally both canister and upright

- ➢ **Webster** – Mop section of store or online
- ➢ **Swifter Floor Mop (Maxi size).** At store or online
- ➢ **Swiffer dusters** (w/extension handle) Any store
- ➢ **Divided caddy** – This is simply for convenience, Target
- ➢ **Plastic pitcher** – Any size over 1.5 quarts, everywhere
- ➢ **Ladder/step stool** – How tall you are and what you have in your house will determine the sizes you'll need
- ➢ **Tool kit** – You need a few screwdrivers and needle nose pliers.
- ➢ **Shower Curtain** (preferably new)
- ➢ **BUCKET – FORBIDDEN** So throw yours out

The Path

Tear this page out to help you follow The PATH while cleaning the BIG JOB and Maintenance until you get the process down.

1. Top to bottom

2. Take it DOWN and Take it OUT? (BIG JOB only)

3. A slice at a time (don't bite off more than you can chew)

4. Back to front

5. Move in ONE DIRECTION – there is no going back!

6. What's in the middle?

7. Finish the floor and you're out!

Breinigsville, PA USA
20 February 2011

255960BV00002B/1/P